THIRD AGE CAREERS

THIRD AGE CAREERS

Meeting the Corporate Challenge

Barry Curnow
and
John McLean Fox

with Eddie Blass

Gower

© Barry Curnow and John McLean Fox 1994

Published by
Gower Publishing Limited
Gower House
Croft Road
Aldershot
Hampshire GU11 3HR
England

Gower
Old Post Road
Brookfield
Vermont 05036
USA

Barry Curnow and John McLean Fox have asserted their right under the Copyright, Designs and Patents Act 1988 to be identified as the joint authors of this work.

British Library Cataloguing in Publication Data
Curnow, Barry
   Third Age Careers: Meeting the Corporate Challenge
   I. Title   II. Fox, John McLean
   658.3132

ISBN 0–566–07493–1

Library of Congress Cataloguing-in-Publication Data
Curnow, Barry
   Third Age Careers: Meeting the Corporate Challenge/ Barry Curnow and John McLean Fox, with Eddie Blass.
      p. cm.
   Includes bibliographical references and index.
   ISBN 0–566–07493–1: $48.95 (est.)
   1. Age and employment.   2. Middle age persons – Employment.   3. Age and employ-ment – Case studies.   4. Middle aged persons – Employment – Case studies.   I. Fox, John McLean.   II. Title.
HD6279.C87   1994
331.3'94 – dc20   94–9878 CIP

Typeset in 10 point Garamond Light by Poole Typesetting (Wessex) Limited and printed in Great Britain at the University Press, Cambridge.

CONTENTS

LIST OF TABLES AND FIGURES

FOREWORD
By Professor Charles Handy

❖

'*Tempora mutantur, et nos mutamur in illis*' – times change and we change with them. So wrote Harrison in his *Description of Britain* in 1577. As it was then, so it is now, four hundred years later; we have to change as the times change, like it or not.

I was in my late forties when I realized that I was going to have to change if I was to fit the times ahead. I was, it seemed, running out of jobs. I had got as far as I was going to get in my chosen profession. Even if I wanted to mark time for fifteen more years in my present role, it was extremely unlikely that I would be allowed to do so. Younger people were both cheaper and more up to date, and huffing and puffing about age discrimination was not going to change that basic fact. I concluded that I would have to rethink my assumptions about my career, my way of life and, crucially, my finances if I wanted life to go on being an interesting and rewarding experience.

I did not know it then, but I was planning for my Third Age, for that period of life beyond the career job and parenting which can last for anything up to thirty years. It was not going to be retirement – I had no wish to be idle for that long and certainly could not afford to be. There had to be work, but it clearly was not going to be the sort of full-time work I had been accustomed to. I was going to have to be much more self-sufficient. There would be no one drawing up career plans for me, arranging training courses or even booking tickets. More worrying than that, however, was my discovery that I would have to sit down and think what sort of life I wanted. I had become conditioned to weekday jobs, annual pay rises and annual holidays. Success had meant more seniority and more money. I had been compiling a curriculum vitae but, suddenly, there was no one interested in looking at it. What was life about, I asked myself, when a c.v. no longer mattered?

I felt that I was looking out on to a wide uncharted sea, one on which I would, in honesty, have preferred not to venture. I can't pretend that the voyage I then embarked on was all easy going but it has been interesting. In retrospect, more than ten years on, I would not have had it otherwise. I now know that the Third Age is not a euphemism for old age or even for retirement. It is a new way of life, one with more choices and more problems, a chance to do and be something different, but also a challenge to cope with. I now know, too, that it is a stage in life which will happen to almost every one of us, because if we reach fifty in reasonable health we are unlikely to die before we are in our late seventies yet will increasingly be leaving our career jobs in our fifties. That gap is the Third Age and before too long nearly one third of all adults will be in it.

Some changes are cyclical: they reverse themselves. This one won't. Organizations will need fewer and shorter career posts as they strip themselves down for a more technological age. At the same time, most of us are, I trust, going to live even more healthily for longer. The gap between the end of the job and the start of senility gets bigger. We shall have to change our picture of life's normal course to fit these changing times and stop deluding ourselves that it won't happen to us. When we take that on board we will realize that it is only common sense to prepare for this Third Age more seriously and more realistically. That is true for the individual but it is also true for the organization. The sensible organization will want to find a way to continue to draw on the experience and skills of its people even when it can't afford to keep them on the full-time payroll. The decent organization will want to help its people make the best use of this unexpected gift of time.

This book, therefore, is made for our times. It is badly needed. I hope that it will sit, open, on many a boardroom table as well as on the personnel manager's desk, for the issues it discusses are the stuff of strategy. To drift into the Third Age is a sure way of discovering the problems without the opportunities. Not only will that be expensive, it will damage any reputation as a preferred employer. I wish only that it had been available to me, and to my employers, when I first set out on that uncharted sea a decade or more ago. Nor could I have wished for better pilots than the two authors of this book. They bring with them long experience of the subject, an active involvement in counselling both individuals and organizations, and much insight into what is needed. We have much to learn, both from them and from the best practices which they describe.

PREFACE

❖

Recent years have seen a shift in the pattern of living which will affect the future of every man, woman and child in Europe. The shift we are talking about is in the period when people enter the second half of life. Their lives thereafter are likely to be quite different from that of their parents or grandparents. At one end of the scale their mainstream working life is likely to cease in their 40s, 50s or 60s; at the other end, they are likely to be more healthy and active than their fore-bears, until they are 75 or 80.

This emerging phase of life is frequently referred to as the 'Third Age', and it is this period that is the focus of this book. The First Age is the period of childhood and education, and the Second Age that of careers, marriage and parenting. The Fourth Age is the final phase – dependency, decline and, ultimately, death.

The father of one of the authors retired at 63, became ill and died at 67. He, in effect, had no Third Age, and that pattern was by no means unusual twenty years ago. The conventional view of life, which is deeply entrenched, is that you should work hard all your life until the day when the paradise of retirement beckons, and it will then, in theory, have all seemed worthwhile. The pension earned is seen as a reward for a lifetime of vigorous effort, and images of a world cruise, deck-chairs in the sun and a permanently tranquil existence crowd the mind.

Reality is not normally like that, however. Many people, in the depths of their being, resent retirement, whether early or not. They put a brave face on it, but consider it a massive rejection of their personal worth, and are fearful of what life might bring in the years to come. They soon discover that the allure of leisure has its limitations (rather like being on holiday with the family for two or three weeks; it can be restful and renewing, but cannot continue for ever). People start to wonder what they are now going to do with their lives. Many miss the security of the workplace boundaries, and the camaraderie of the extended family of colleagues. ICI were one of the first companies to recognise that life expectancy after retirement at normal retirement age could be as little as 2 years.

We decided to write this book to help companies and individuals to understand that Third Age existence can be stimulating and fulfilling, if viewed and acted upon in the right way.

Specifically, our aims in writing are to:

O   outline the implications of the Third Age phenomenon as a business issue for organizations and as a critical life-planning requirement for individuals

O   help create an awareness of the opportunity for and the significance of a positive approach to Third Age planning and living

O   put forward practical ways in which businesses can enhance the motivation and performance of mature employees

O   indicate how individuals can plan their future in such a way that they will experience a fulfilled Third Age

O   share our experiences gained during the build up of the Third Age consultancy firm, Future Perfect.

A significant impression from our research and personal experience is that few people in the Second Age appreciate fully the implications of making a transition to the Third Age. Many people view the employment of Third Agers using Second Age criteria. Managers tend to distance themselves from the issues involved until they approach middle life themselves. Then, if they begin to acknowledge the fact of an impending personal transition within the next decade, and if they prepare for it, they may thrive and prosper. If they ignore and deny the Third Age, however, they may be doomed to a dreary or even painful one. In other words, people rarely understand that they need to use fundamentally different criteria to examine Third Age living, compared with the features that are important in the main career phase.

There is a significant obstacle to achieving a necessary shift in attitudes, since the younger executives with appropriate authority have little personal or emotional involvement with Third Age issues, whilst older executives are trying to avoid the topic (as it is almost 'too close for comfort'). The recession of the early 1990s has engendered a great deal of fear and distress, since in that climate redundancy and early retirement have in many instances led to an abrupt change of circumstances. We believe that individuals should take greater control over their lives and careers, and should be encouraged to take an independent route early on, in their 40s or early 50s. We envisage a future in which companies will manage their businesses with a much more flexible resourcing policy, calling on people as and when the need arises, rather than creating a rigid, all-embracing establishment. If such a change can be achieved successfully, it will be of benefit both to companies, which will operate more cost effectively, and to individuals, who will become more resourceful, in the complete sense of the word. The big challenge to overcome, however, is the TRANSITION from one situation and world view, as an employee, to another markedly different one, as a freelance agent, member of a specialist grouping, or participating in other arrangements of productive endeavours for the Third Age.

This book examines the facts of the Third Age, the challenge that it represents for companies, the feelings that it evokes in individuals, and the prospects for taking control and managing the transitions involved. In doing so we have drawn on not only our own experience but that of leading organizations who are attempting to develop practical solutions as good employers.

We would like to acknowledge, with much gratitude, the research and help provided by Eddie Blass, with her remarkable enthusiasm for the topic. Despite her relative youth, she has shown an understanding of Third Age transition well beyond her years. We would also like to pay tribute to John Ottensooser, without whom this book would not have been written, to Charles Handy, for his unfailing personal encouragement, and to our other friends, colleagues and clients associated with the Future Perfect venture. Finally, we are indebted to our long-suffering wives, Penny and Maria, for their generous support and insight.

Barry Curnow

John McLean Fox

PART I

THIRD AGE TRANSITION

❖

1
THE CONTEXT

❖

An American visiting England asked 'why is it that over here whenever I ask the reason for anything, any institution or ceremony or set of rules, they always give me an historical answer?' The Europeans, suggests Professor Charles Handy, look backwards to the best of their history and change as little as they can, while Americans look forward and want to change as much as possible.

Yet attitudes to people over 40 in the workplace have not changed much in the US, let alone in the UK and Europe. For example, there tends to be a general misconception that you are too old once you are over 40 when applying for a job. In the UK we have legislation that prevents discrimination on the grounds of race, gender, marital status, etc. but not age. Why are so many executives allowed to retire at their desks in dead-end jobs for the last ten years or so of their main careers?

Issues relating to mature employees are becoming increasingly important, and the Carnegie Inquiry into 'Life, Work and Livelihood in the Third Age' reviewed such aspects in an important study carried out between 1990 and 1993. One of the main reasons for this study was the absence of a statistical map concerning facts related to the Third Age in the UK. Historical demographic data appeared to focus on the First, Second, and Fourth ages, i.e. on the periods covering childhood/ education, work/marriage, retirement/decline. Consequently, at the upper end of the age scale, people were either considered to be working (up to 60 for women and 65 for men) or retired/declining. The Third Age category, i.e. those between ages 50 and 75, had not been identified statistically because the segment had not yet become significant; the Inquiry subsequently found that in the UK there would be some 15 million people in their Third Age in the year 2000 (or 25.4 per cent of the total population of 59.1 million) rising to 18.5 million in 2020 (or 30.4 per cent of 60.8 million). The equivalent number in the US is forecast to be about 33 per cent at this time; these are surely highly significant segments of the population.

It is interesting to look at this situation in a little more depth, and into the implications for employment. There are several demographic changes we should note in this context.

3

DEMOGRAPHIC CHANGES

FEWER BABIES

The birth rate in Europe fell dramatically in the 1970s and has continued downwards. If fewer people are born now, then there will be fewer women to have children in the future, and so on. In addition, as more and more women are entering or re-entering the labour market to pursue careers they are opting either not to have a family or to start a family later in life. *Figure 1.1* indicates the trend in the number of children per couple in each member state of the European Community and highlights the relatively rapid rate of decline since 1960. The average for the 12 countries is a decline from 2.63 to 1.58 children per couple in only 29 years, a decrease of 39.9 per cent or 1.4 per cent per year. We are not even reproducing ourselves at the present time.

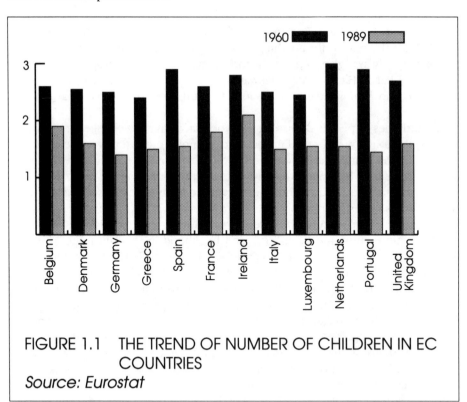

FIGURE 1.1   THE TREND OF NUMBER OF CHILDREN IN EC
              COUNTRIES
Source: Eurostat

LONGER LIVES

At the same time, the advance of medical science means that we are living longer. Most of our grandparents never knew their grandparents. Most of our parents knew their grandparents, and most of us will know great-grandparents, or at least our children will. Whereas people used only to live until 50 at the turn of the century in the UK (the average being 45 for men, 49 for women), life expectancy for people born in 1991 is 73 for men and 79 for women. With potential breakthroughs for treating people with Altzheimer's disease and senile dementia it may not be long until we continue being sound in mind and body until 100.

It is only within the last two (or at most three) decades, that the Third Age has emerged as a significant feature in our lives. The first annual report of the European Community Observatory drew a comparison between the proportion of the population over 50 years of age in 1990 and 2020 (see *Figure 1.2*). In the UK those who reach 50 can now expect to live until old age, the average for men being 76 and for women 81. The Carnegie Inquiry found that the extra years gained do not generally involve disability, which is a very encouraging feature. The average population percentage for those over 50 in the 12 European countries is a projected rise from 31.3 per cent in 1990 to 42.2 per cent in 2020. Since the population covered has already been born it is likely to be a valid projection.

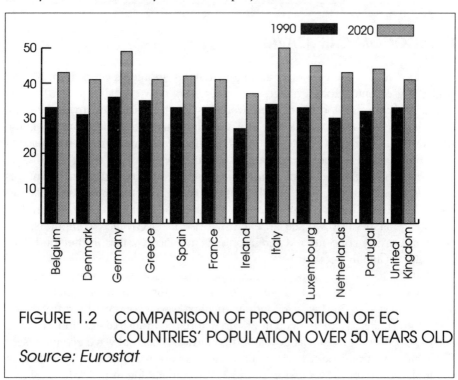

FIGURE 1.2   COMPARISON OF PROPORTION OF EC COUNTRIES' POPULATION OVER 50 YEARS OLD

Source: Eurostat

In the UK, the age structure is predicted to change between 1991 and 2021 as shown in *Table 1.1*. There is a marked shift between the two age ranges, firstly 16 to 49, which declines from 48.5 per cent down to 42.1 per cent, and secondly 50 and over, which increases from 31.2 per cent to 38.5 per cent. An important implication of these trends is a sharp increase in the number of older people of pensionable age in comparison with those of working age. Carnegie predicts a figure of 42 state pensioners per 100 of working age in 2030, compared with the present 30. Similar figures for children *and* pensioners are 79 compared with 63.

Age Group	1991		2021	
	Pop. in millions	%	Pop. in millions	%
Under 16	11.7	20.3	11.8	19.4
16–29	12.3	21.3	11.1	18.3
30–49	15.7	27.2	14.5	23.8
50–74	14.0	24.3	18.5	30.4
75 and over	4.0	6.9	4.9	8.1
Totals	57.7		60.8	

TABLE 1.1   PREDICTED CHANGE OF UK AGE STRUCTURE BETWEEN 1991
AND 2021.
Source: Annual Abstract of Statistics and OPCS

THE ECONOMIC UPHEAVAL

Let us look now at the economic and industrial developments which have accompanied these demographic changes.

During previous depressions there were crises in the basic industries of Britain. Large industries were shut down. The steel industry, shipbuilding and mining, which were the majority employers in many cities, were shut down in the space of a few months and seldom if ever were powerful new industries rising at the same time, though imaginative schemes for job creation were initiated by such ventures as British Steel Industries and British Coal Enterprise. Today the mass-manufacturing industries of textiles, rubber, steel, shipbuilding, auto, etc. are in terminal agony. Simultaneously we see an explosive rise in electronics, computers, etc. which are largely concentrated geographically in 'Silicon Valley' in the South East and 'Silicon Glen' in Scotland.

What has happened has been not so much a recession as a restructuring of the entire technoeconomic base of our society. In the short term we are shifting from a second wave to a third wave economy. In a first wave economy the main institution is the family, as experienced in Britain before the Industrial Revolution and as still experienced in most less developed countries. A second wave economy sees the main institution being corporations and government. This was evident in Britain largely until the recession of the 1970s culminating in the 'Winter of Discontent'. Now we are clearly moving towards a third wave economy (or new age economy) where the main institution is the individual.

Thatcherite policy through the 1980s and now Majorism in the 1990s is breeding a new society. The working class as it was previously known no longer exists, and there are no longer any working-class heroes. Now, there is the working class who are home owners and shareholders, and an underclass who have very little at all, often not even a roof over their head. Education now has to be bought with the advent of student loans and the freezing of grants.

INFORMATION TECHNOLOGY AND ORGANIZATIONAL STRUCTURES

Now we are a society with an economy based on the creation and distribution of information. We have moved from being an industrial society to an information society. The shift started in the mid 1950s. In 1956, for the first time in US history, white-collar workers in technical, managerial and clerical positions outnumbered blue-collar workers. For the first time in history, more people worked with information than were producing goods. It was Harvard sociologist Daniel Bell who coined the name 'post-industrial society' for it. In 1950 17 per cent of the US workforce worked in information jobs; now more than 60 per cent do. Scholars predicted that the post-industrial economy would be based on services but the overwhelming majority of service workers are engaged in the creation, processing and distribution of information. The new source of power is not money in the hands of a few, but information in the hands of the many, and the changes are happening so fast that most of us are running to keep up and even then not always succeeding.

As the changes facing us now are probably as radical as those associated with the Industrial Revolution, the rules for corporate survival have also had to change. Traditional managers have been disposed of. The habits of a lifetime, the very habits that helped build the organizations, are now seen as counter-productive and obsolete. The first rule of survival is that nothing is more dangerous than yesterday's success.

'It will no longer be possible to carry passengers. Those who have failed to live up to their earlier promise must go. Jobs which could be done as well by others younger and usually cheaper must be vacated so that they are available.' Typically this sort of statement was made in almost every large organization and out went the people who had been with the company for some 30 years or so since leaving full-time education. Many were made redundant or were pensioned off early, at great cost to the company. A large amount of money has been spent in paying people to go away and do nothing.

However, what happens when business improves again and companies find that not only do they not have the staff they require, but they also lack the resources to recruit, train, mentor and supervise the new staff that will be coming through the company? Many organizations and institutions are tending to be short termist in this situation. They see the rising unemployment figures and take comfort at the thought that there are many potential recruits out there should they need them. Many of the people available, however, are unskilled and may be of little use to them, whilst those that remain in the organization may not have the knowledge and experience to build up the organization as did many of those who have left.

For better or for worse, organizations have changed. They are flatter rather than hierarchical. They tend to have a smaller central core and contract outsiders to fill any gaps. Many of the middle manager executives who were pushed out in the delayering process return as consultants to fill the areas where their departures have left a gap. Charles Handy's 'Shamrock' organization has emerged as predicted and it calls for a new style of management, for a new age of workers.

The Shamrock organization can perhaps be thought of as piecework rediscovered but in a more effective manner. Such an organization puts a large amount of work out on contract, paying fees for results. A Shamrock organization has a core of precious, essential, hard-working, high salary workers dedicated to the job. Outside this core in support roles are contractors who either do certain routine work such as secretarial services, catering or maintenance work, or act as advisers to the core, working on specific projects and bringing in the knowledge, experience and resources lacking in the core team.

EMPLOYMENT ACTIVITY

The change in UK employment activity rates for those over 55 (some 3.5 million people or 12.4 per cent of the workforce in 1990) – a reduction for men of 22.9 per cent between 1970 and 1988 – is quite startling. There would inevitably be an even greater reduction if current rates were taken into account. A comparison is given in *Table 1.2*. Both France and Germany have promoted early retirement strongly,

	1970 %	1988 %	% Change
UK	91.3	68.4	−22.9
Japan	86.6	82.3	− 4.3
Sweden	85.4	74.9	−10.5
Germany	82.2	56.5	−25.7
US	80.7	66.4	−14.3
France	75.4	47.3	−28.1
Netherlands	72.2	38.5	−33.7

TABLE 1.2   ACTIVITY RATES FOR MEN AGED 55–64 YEARS
Source: OECD Activity Statistics (1989)

whereas Sweden and the US have taken active measures to encourage the employment of older workers; the US has introduced a framework of protection of workers' rights which prohibits discrimination on the grounds of age and provides payment of damages if found to have occurred. There is thus considerable need and scope for promoting the active employment of older workers in the majority of countries.

The Carnegie Inquiry drew attention to various trends in UK employment in the 1990s and beyond, of which the following are the most prominent:

O   We could be moving towards an increasing proportion of part-time, casual and self-employed jobs filled disproportionately by women and older men.

Concern is expressed in the Carnegie Report that this form of employment should follow a high value-added route, embracing relevant training and skills development, rather than a low wage, low value-added route.

O   Employers are unlikely to reappraise policies towards older workers in the immediate future, in view of a relatively weak economic demand. However, in the longer term these policies are likely to change as the baby boom generation retires and the marked shift referred to earlier becomes more evident.

O   This shift has drawn attention to the requirement for adequate training and work experience for the baby boom generation to prepare for the future, more highly-skilled economy.

The study found a widespread use of age bars in recruitment advertisements, use of age as a selection criterion, and a greater emphasis on attributes associated with younger people, even for jobs where the characteristics attributed to older people may be more important. It was considered that this practice could be against the best interests of the individual firm as well as against the interests of older workers. The capabilities identified by the health study show that age is not a good indicator of the ability to work and learn. In addition, older people are likely to leave less quickly once recruited. A main conclusion has been that employers tend to operate on the basis of a stereotyped image, and are still concentrating on prime age, full-time employees.

EDUCATION AND THE FUTURE WORKFORCE

In 1986 McKinsey predicted that 70 per cent of all jobs in Europe would require cerebral skills rather than manual skills by the year 2000, with 35 per cent needing a higher education or professional qualification to be carried out adequately. Hence 35 per cent of all age groups (a conservative estimate) should be entering higher education. Currently only 18 per cent of school leavers are entering higher education. This is a rise from 14 per cent in 1988, but this rise is not because of an increase in the number entering higher education, but because of a fall in the number of people in the age group. The UK trend is for over 40 per cent of school leavers to leave school without a GCSE in one subject. This does not represent an optimistic state of affairs.

Because there will be a relative shortage of youth in the future it is imperative that the youth that we do have are adequately skilled to fill the vacancies. Clearly they are unlikely to have such skills in the short term; the phenomenon of youth unemployment is unlikely to disappear. In fact there is likely to be a continuing predicament in which those who leave school unqualified cannot find suitable employment for the whole of what would be their anticipated normal working life.

So where will the skilled labour come from?

NEW WAYS OF WORKING

The new labour force will in part emerge from the 5 million inactive women over 25, and those in their late 50s and 60s who might otherwise retire. It is estimated that an additional 80 000 women in the UK will join organizations in the next eight years. Many of them will be well educated and qualified. The women themselves will be exercising their choice, doing what they want to do, but they will need appropriate pay and conditions if the right results are to be attained.

Organizations are likely to be squeezed by the need for all the intelligent qualified people they can get, and by the shortage of well-educated, qualified youngsters. Overall there is likely to be a significant skills shortage. As technology continually advances, and what was new a year ago is obsolete now, there will be a need for continual training. On the other hand, many jobs will disappear as electronic systems take over, and many jobs will be simplified so that they can be completed by less skilled labour. Computer programming, for example, used to involve skill in the use of binary numbers. Now, anyone can buy an off-the-shelf database package and use it for programming. It is still necessary to have skills to be effective, but the degree of skill necessary has decreased. Sooner or later there will be self-writing programs where you simply tell the computer what you want from what information and it will write the program for you.

With the advent of modems and the added sophistication of two people being able to work on the same document simultaneously (such that a change that one person makes is transferred down a telephone line to the other person's terminal and the change appears on their VDU also), we will also see the age of the telecommuter. With the help of technological interconnections, remote work sites will be scattered worldwide. This will cut down on office space and eliminate long drives to work, easing some of the congestion problems currently faced in inner cities.

Research shows that disciplined employees who work at home put in more hours on the job with less absenteeism and greater longevity with the company. However, it does not suit everyone. Some people miss the interaction and office gossip and find the high-tech isolation unbearable. Others prefer the attractions of not having to travel to work, and having the comfort of working from their own home. Provided an appropriate level of face-to-face interaction is combined with this somewhat isolated activity, this format has considerable potential, we believe. The FI Group, founded by Steve Shirley in the 1960s, was based on 'distributed office' techniques, and the majority of staff worked from their homes. The company now employs 1 000 people and has an annual turnover of £30m. By the end of the century a substantial proportion of the working population could be operating in this way.

Those people who know how to manage the Third Age employee and who understand the third wave economy structure will be in great demand in the workplace. Whilst many industries are suffering a decline, others are excelling in productivity and growth. Those businesses which are successful are likely to be the information-based, knowledge-powered and capital intensive research and development companies. Some industries have chosen to move forward from second wave status by computerizing assembly lines, developing creative labour union contracts, diversifying into new products and services, frequently closing down or acquiring new businesses. Others have tried to raise capital, cut wages, renegotiate labour contracts to keep doing what they have always done, and in the process are rendering themselves extinct. Many organizations have not yet started to consider fully what the challenges ahead may mean for them, and how they might address them.

In a third wave economy such as ours, the most valuable resource is time. We will see rapid service cycling and short shelf-lives. Products, social institutions, people and careers will come and go at rapid rates. There will be no job security, increased job obsolescence, extensive new product development with a high degree of product failure, and production speed and effectiveness will be valued increasingly. Worlds perceived as safe havens in the past are becoming perilous, as the work systems of former times become unacceptable. The effect on individuals will be marked, as people become confused and question where they will find their security and prosperity.

As the basic economic unit becomes the individual, organizations will begin to encourage their employees to take a firm control of their career, finances and lifestyle. There will be a move towards freedom of movement and creativity, as the new generations are already starting to turn their backs on old style authoritative management. People are seeking independence now more than ever before. More and more people want to be their own boss, including Third Agers. Many Third Agers are looking forward to their retirement so that they can finally have the freedom to do what they want and perhaps set up on their own. Those who will succeed will be the people with significant know-how, information and networks. Specialists will prosper in the new economy. Ultimately, anyone who cannot make a unique contribution might well be replaced by a robot or some other form of automated process. Those who anticipate and respond to the new economic conditions should be able to reap great rewards, whilst those that don't will be left by the wayside.

For the first time, probably since the Industrial Revolution if not before, individuals will have the opportunity to shape their work to suit the way they want to live, rather than suffer their lifestyles to be dictated by their jobs. With so many home workers telecommuting to central offices, choice and individual freedom will prevail, though work of poor quality will receive poorer rewards, and a job done well will be well rewarded. For those who are unable to keep up with the pace of change there will be a tremendous amount of stress, which will impact directly on home life, marriages, families, etc. It is predicted that many people will opt for part-time work as a way of reducing stress and increasing quality time with their families. The disadvantage of this would be lower earnings, but the choice will belong to the individual rather than the company. In June 1991, 25 per cent of the British workforce were working part time, with over 5 million part-time workers, 90 per cent of whom are women.

Before the 1970s recession, people left college and normally joined a company where they stayed until the day they retired, the 'cradle to grave' syndrome. The economic uncertainties of the 1970s started to erode the 'job for life' mentality. Fifty years ago managers changed companies once in their working life. Now the average is seven times in a working lifetime. By the year 2000 this may no longer be a feature, since many workers could lead a portfolio lifestyle, working for several companies at the same time on a freelance contract basis during their 'main career' phase.

THE UPWARDLY AND DOWNWARDLY MOBILE PROFESSIONALS

Those people who understand and know how to deal with change will be the survivors in the new economy. We know a young woman who finished her first degree two years ago. Now she works full time on flexible hours to allow part-time study for her second degree. She has already decided what her third degree will be, and is gradually becoming very specialised in her field. She invested in her own computer and continually tries to learn how to use new computer programs. As a result she understands how computers think and troubleshoots for companies who get stuck at a fairly basic level, sometimes using packages she has never been trained on or necessarily used before. Her parents worry that she is going to be a student for the rest of her life. However, she sees that mode of existence as the only way forward. At a time when so much is changing it is important to keep up to date, to read journals, to study new work methods and to be a specialist. At the age of 23 this young woman successfully leads a portfolio lifestyle and has greater demands on her time than she has time available. She appreciates that change is continual and does not wait for people to catch up with it. She is clearly an upwardly mobile professional.

Another feature of this progressively competitive environment is the extent to which an MBA has become an essential requirement for the upwardly mobile executive in industry or commerce. Launched in the UK in only three centres in the mid-1960s (there are now 100 courses available), the MBA programme is now a recognized step for a junior executive to take if he or she wishes to advance their career significantly. Though only a means to an end, rather than an end in itself, the MBA's current popularity demonstrates a rapid turnabout compared with the scepticism prevalent in the 1970s. An MBA from Insead, Harvard, Stanford or one of the key UK business schools is now regarded as a passport to success, and students are consequently prepared to fund themselves the £10 000 or so required.

Compare these two categories of individual with a downwardly mobile professional, generally born before 1950, who refuses to acknowledge the need to update and change. Our examples might not have the experience of the pre-1950 worker, but they are anticipating change and are therefore in step with the economy rather than three steps behind it. They are typical of the new generation of young individualistic capitalists and entrepreneurs that are gradually being developed in a more open and changing culture.

However, turning back to a previous issue, there are unlikely to be sufficient of these enlightened people to go round, and the number available will decrease year by year. So is it not time to start reconsidering personnel policies so that they will cater for the available labour force rather than the perceived ideal? Those in the Third Age present employers with significant opportunities for cost-effective resourcing, which this book will explore in greater depth.

2
ORGANIZATIONS AND THE THIRD AGE

❖

The authors, through Future Perfect, launched two specific research projects to review Third Age issues, the first being completed in 1991, the second in 1992. The objective of both pieces of research was to review the policies and practice of companies in this field, and to discover how they viewed the issues involved. In addition, special studies were carried out for a number of large corporations during this period, which provided a unique insight into the attitudes of organizations and their employees on these topics. The findings of this research, reported under separate headings in chronological order, are given below.

1991 'THE MANAGEMENT AND EMPLOYMENT OF PEOPLE AGED 45 PLUS'

INTRODUCTION

The study arose as a result of discussions at a research forum mounted by Future Perfect in July 1990. Personnel directors from a number of leading organizations put forward their initial reactions to the Third Age issues identified from previous research. This forum enabled participants to express their concerns freely on such subjects as the potential shortage of younger entrants, the possible shift to an older age distribution and the motivation of mature managers and employees.

The priority concerns expressed at that time were:

O   the difficulties inherent in managing organizational change sufficiently flexibly, so that specific Third Agers can be motivated and then released

O   the dichotomy between the needs of the organization with those of individual employees, and the reconciliation necessary

13

O   the most appropriate response to meet the emerging demographic changes

O   the practical aspect of enabling Third Agers to change role or leave without 'loss of face'; status and self-esteem were recognized to be disproportionately important to them

O   the potentially adverse impact on younger employees if the company did not 'get it right' for older people.

Consequently, the study was mounted within nine large corporations during October through to February to address these and other issues. One participant joined in the study because he confessed that 'we just haven't got a policy for dealing with older people'. In the event, this was true for the majority of participants.

The objectives of the study were:

> To provide participating companies with a sound basis for enabling them to develop an enhanced human resources policy with respect to Third Age issues through reviewing the ways in which companies are addressing these issues, and to highlight the practical implications for management.

The interviews were carried out within nine companies across the UK (British Gas, BUPA, Guinness, Kleinwort Benson, Legal and General, London Underground, National Westminster Bank, Nuclear Electric, Woolwich Building Society), and covered some 130 employees in total. The aim was to achieve as balanced a representation as possible, and the coverage extended functionally, geographically and hierarchically to suit the particular organization's circumstances. Each interview lasted a minimum of one hour; there was a willingness to help and to speak openly, so we felt we were able to gain a true insight into the culture of the different companies and their human resource priorities in this area.

There are two categories of findings, i.e. business issues on the one hand and the impact on employees on the other. They are described separately below.

BUSINESS ISSUES RELATED TO HUMAN RESOURCES

The organizations participating in the study are involved in very different business areas. One would not expect, therefore, that the business issues relating to human resources (HR) would show a great deal of similarity. To our surprise, however, we found a markedly common thread of issues and priorities across the companies. Frequently we were able to cross-reference situations between the different organizations, which helped to give us a greater insight into that particular category.

One feature that emerged very strongly during the study was the *business* significance of the Third Age issues. The idea that the topic of 'older workers' is peripheral to business activities, and restricted to appropriate welfare provision, was knocked firmly on the head. One might even go further and claim that, in view of the potential shortage of younger entrants, the way in which mature employees are managed and motivated (as a significant proportion of the total HR investment) is very much a business priority.

The common themes that emerged from our interviews and widespread discussions are described below.

Managing change

A preoccupation with the majority of senior managers is the effective management of rapid, continuing change. An overriding concern was expressed at the rate at which change was occurring; many thought that changes were in hand that were greater than the organization could expect to digest. The reality, however, is that the business imperatives driving those organizations forward necessitate such a degree of change; it is an integral part of business life. Charles Handy in his book *The Age of Unreason*, Century Hutchison, 1989, points out that we have moved from an environment of continuous change to one of discontinuous change, which is more difficult to manage because it is so much less predictable.

One interviewee summed up his priority objective as being:

> Managing change, to ensure optimum motivation of those involved, and to improve financial performance during this process.

Another interviewee commented:

> We are trying to manage difficult cultural change so that people *know* you are consciously managing change; through a sensitive responsiveness coupled with commercialism.

Two particular features of structural change appeared to be important in the HR context.

Devolution to business units Typically a central organization has been split into a headquarters function with separate business units or profit centres. There were some organizations in our study which had, unwittingly, turned themselves into a 'loose federation' of companies, some of which had virtually rejected corporate allegiance. This appeared to have an adverse effect on the motivation of mature employees, who found their activities restricted to their own unit and they had ceased to have any contact with the rest of the organization. In terms of career development this lack of breadth and mobility can create a negative situation. One organization realized that too much had been devolved, and certain functions, such as succession planning, were now being pulled back. Devolution has many merits, but the total human resource planning implications require careful consideration if adverse fragmentation features are to be avoided.

Relevant quotes:

> We are trying to move too fast, there is a lack of integrated working with everyone trying to achieve a common goal.

> The focus on business units means less contact throughout the company and hinders career moves

Diversification/acquisition Most successful businesses are either diversifying or making acquisitions in a very significant way. These moves tend to place a considerable strain on human resource planning; there are never enough of the right sort of people at the time of a major diversification or acquisition.

As one executive commented:

> We will need younger, flexible executives who will be able to interpret and assess corporate/country cultures and implement the necessary restructuring following an acquisition. We will also need wise, experienced people to help sort out the wheat from the chaff.

Cost effectiveness

In the current economic climate all businesses are reviewing costs, and are looking for both radical and incremental means of gearing up their cost effectiveness. This has a direct impact on staffing levels and HR planning; consequently a large proportion of employees, regardless of age or status, are concerned for their jobs at the present time. This is a feature, however, which will always be with us to some degree and there is a continuing need for improvements in cost effectiveness to be achieved.

One person interviewed summarized it thus:

> The need to cut costs, however, is the driving force at the present time, and payroll costs are the most significant item. There is pressure to reduce staff numbers through technology and rationalization, and 45 to 55 year olds will bear the brunt of redundancy.

Another put it more succinctly:

> To survive the company must reduce numbers.

There are two particular features of cost-effectiveness moves which should perhaps be mentioned in this connection.

Downsizing/delayering   The most common approach to reducing staff numbers in a radical way is to remove an organizational layer. Though sometimes seen as an end in itself, it is very much in tune with the trend towards individual operators, flatter structures and flexible teams.

The management squeeze   Moves which reduce staff numbers frequently add yet another burden on senior and middle managers. A lack of adequate man-management is identified as a serious weakness later in this chapter; fewer numbers tend to mean that pressures on every individual increases, particularly the already stressed manager. Consequently, this and other 'soft' features are ignored, so that motivation suffers.

One comment is relevant:

> Though we are growing, our structures have become much flatter, so that there are few chances for promotion upwards, only sideways. How should we motivate the relevant managers? Motivating mature people and enabling them to perform is a major issue.

Value from the HR investment

Coincidental with moves to improve cost effectiveness by reducing staff numbers and eliminating organizational layers, there is a need to achieve optimum value from the company's HR investment. To assess this it will be necessary to determine the cost benefit of employing different groups of people (by age, type, grade) to address future needs. There are three particular elements in this situation.

Scarce skills   An essential feature of effective HR planning is the identification of scarce skills. Time and again we are told of specialist staff groups which were in desperately short supply; frequently, a host company would train employees in new skills themselves, to find them snapped up by a competitor shortly afterwards. As an example:

> We are *already* employing too many agency staff (1 in 4) and are short of good quality engineers; where are they going to come from?

Flexibility/structures/teams   We have already touched on some of the implications of flatter structures. A key ingredient of the new arrangements should be *flexibility*, so that optimum benefit can be obtained from groupings and regroupings of multi-skill employees of different ages, grades and cost. This is particularly relevant to the effective utilization of mature employees in the future.

A relevant comment was:

> There's a great drive to change the style of operation and culture, to open up the organization to be freer and franker; to be flatter and with wider responsibilities ... and downsized.

Redeployment/retraining   It is evident that there should be a benefit from redeploying a competent employee, in which the company has already invested, rather than to lose him or her. All too frequently, however, this does not appear to be practised widely and it is an area of potential opportunity for mature employees, assuming the company is able to plan accordingly.

Unfortunately the experience of one interviewee is relevant:

> Fifty-five and above are chosen as the first tranche for redeployment; they are often the wrong ones to go.

Performance/profit

In a number of the organizations covered there was a new commercialism apparent. Whether or not the organization was considered to be 'commercial' previously, there appeared to be a concerted focus on individual, business unit and corporate performance which was sharper than before. This naturally affects HR aspects directly, not only from the cost point of view already covered, but also the pay, motivation, personal achievement and assessment factors.

The implications for employees, and particularly mature ones, are illustrated in the following:

> The company has a morale problem with uncertainty; no one knows where they are going and it is very unsettling. People in their early 50s cannot see any career opportunities ahead, which is very different from 10 to 15 years ago, when the situation at age 60 could have been predicted.

and

> In our profit centre (under pressure) we have to be flexible and responsive to market needs; the attitude of 'job for life' should be changed, therefore, and job security related to performance.

and

> The emphasis on performance-related pay has the result of easing out people; we no longer have job security.

Other main changes

Two other issues which impact on human resources have been identified during our study.

Technology   The main feature of technology developments is that they never stop; technology now affects nearly every part of an organization to a greater or lesser degree, and it is not just a 'once-off' injection. One interviewee, in relation to the effect of this on mature employees, commented rather cynically:

> Increasingly people will begin to be found out as technology becomes a main force in life; younger people will overtake older.

It is inevitable that some developments will be difficult for older people to cope with; it is not only the particular technology or system that is being used, but the continuing nature and pace of change. This aspect has to be taken into account in our HR planning.

Customer/contractor   As part of total quality management initiatives there is an increasing emphasis on supply chain relationships, and the fact that everyone is both a customer and a contractor, internally and externally. This philosophy is sometimes difficult for mature employees to recognize and practice. One interviewee talked about the difficulties involved in generating a culture 'in which we think about service, and recovering every penny we spend … which can be harder for older people, especially those furthest from the ultimate customer'.

IMPACT ON 45 PLUS EMPLOYEES

In this section we explore the impact on mature employees of the business issues mentioned earlier. This will be considered both from the *management* point of view, in the context of organizational and management implications, and the *individual* aspect, related to the personal responses and insights we gained. The topic is broken down as follows.

Generalizations on age are false

During the course of the study we came to realize that to talk about employees aged 45 plus as a cohesive group was quite artificial. Though there is a similarity in aspects related to the ageing process, such as physical mobility and speed of reaction, it would not be valid to generalize on competence, skills capability or other such qualities. One senior manager put it this way: 'There are young 50s and there are old 50s.'

It is a point with which most of us would agree, but few tend to recognize this feature in practice in the employment situation, it would appear. There was only one organization we met which could comfortably give an impression of age not being a significant or slightly shameful factor. In the equal opportunities context, 'older employees' issues are following 'women' issues as the next target. Generalization can lead to older employees being seen as a problem rather than an opportunity, and inappropriate measures taken. We support moves to increase awareness of positive age implications, however, and commend the Institute of Personnel Management (IPM) for their recent statement on age and employment, and the initiatives being taken by Age Resource and the Third Age Network.

At the risk of further generalization there appear to be certain features which can be recognized in a 'Young 50' and others in an 'Old 50'.

Young 50s want to be part of it   We met a number of 'younger' mature managers who felt frustrated and were very keen to contribute fully to their company's current development. Here the attitude of companies is generally very discouraging to older people, as instanced by the following verbatim comments:

> My impression is that age 40 to 45 is the ceiling for promotion; I would expect a 35-year old to get the job. It's as though they think you wake up on your 45th birthday and your brain's gone.

> 45 plus staff are not wanted or valued.

> People aged 45 plus are seen to be 'over the hill'.

> Older people now retire early, the average age has dropped by ten years in the past ten years.

> There is a promotion ceiling at 45 and the age is coming down.

It is hardly surprising, therefore, to find a feeling of frustration and disquiet among the more competent mature managers and employees, who feel that they could be used to greater advantage.

One person commented:

> I don't know what's happening. I would like to contribute to sorting things out and the whole question of a proper balance and fit of people.

Old 50s cannot cope   At the other end of the scale, we came across a considerable number of mature employees who no longer wished to participate in new developments, and who were either just working for their pension or, in some cases, wanted to change jobs or leave. The majority of Old 50s felt insecure and anxious about the future, as illustrated by the following comments:

> A hit list exists for many aged 50 plus.

> The current perception is 'we need young people to change this company', which is dangerous.

> Some people are less able to cope as they grow older, but they are 'looked after'; can this practice apply in the future?

> We've been shedding older people too quickly, we should control it and not allow it to happen so fast.

The worst feature about the Old 50s in quite a few organizations is that those who had not progressed (usually 'stuck' in junior, or possibly, middle management) were acting as a serious blockage to organizational developments. This aspect, almost more than any other, seemed to indicate the need for a new approach in organizations where this applied.

> We are undergoing a major culture change, older people (middle managers in their 40s and 50s) are unable to take the change and are a stumbling block.

Craving for personal attention

Apart from some senior managers, who felt relatively independent and secure, there was a universal craving for personal attention. It is a paradox that mature, grown-up men and women (who might be expected not to have such a foible) have a strong desire for recognition, appreciation and other forms of attention, yet it is a reality. These are just a few of many similar comments:

> I feel like a cog in a massive machine.

> We are taken for granted and held in *current* roles because of value to the company.

> I suspect my boss doesn't know whether or not I am married or have any children.

Without going into the psychological aspects in any depth, it does appear that people's values change in mid-life and they can frequently move from being 'outer-directed', i.e. concerned with visible success and related material gains, to becoming more 'inner-directed' i.e. intent on the less tangible qualities of fulfilment, in career and family life, exploring new fields and seeking a spiritual dimension.

One of the main findings from this study is that there is frequently *a lack of an open dialogue between the organization and the employees on their future career and personal values*. Though some organizations make use of the performance appraisal process to cover wider career issues there is rarely the opportunity for the employee to explore, openly and honestly, his or her personal values and aspirations and to discuss how the company sees that person's future career.

New structures and roles

The new, flatter structures require a modified management style and different roles for the manager and his or her subordinates. This change away from conventional hierarchies is often difficult for the mature employee to take, particularly if a former manager now becomes a consultant. The aspects we would draw attention to are that:

O   new structures demand different roles, and facilitation of the role change for mature employees will require careful handling
O   a change of role for mature employees is one of the means of giving them a new lease of life, properly orchestrated
O   managing a flat 'washing line' requires *direction* rather than *supervision*.

Transition models

In most downsizing programmes there is a presumption that employees aged 50 plus will be 'the first to go'. We suggest, based on the evidence of our study, that this might be an unwise course of action to take. The main factor is that a whole raft of experience can disappear at a stroke, to be regretted subsequently. We were told of a number of instances where such hasty action had been taken, and certain individuals called back to fulfil their roles as mentors.

In addition, such a solution may well be expensive, compared with releasing younger, less competent people who would cost much less in terms of severance arrangements. All in all, the benefits of retaining a balanced age profile would appear to be considerable. Transition of mature employees therefore represents both a problem and an opportunity. As a problem, it is something that has to be managed effectively, which few companies have yet achieved with sufficient sensitivity and flexibility. As an opportunity, it is a feature which can be a positive part of an organization's human resources policy, particularly if a creative approach to phased retirement can be initiated (so that experienced employees can still be available when required).

1992 'BUSINESS AND WORK IN MID-LIFE

A second piece of research was initiated on specific topics to gain further information and to assess company attitudes to relevant initiatives in this field. The research reviewed corporate approaches to mid-life planning for employees, and complemented Future Perfect's sponsored research with individuals, carried out by the British Market Research Bureau. The results suggested that many company recruitment policies, ages and conditions tended to be out of date and inappropriate for dealing with Third Age challenges in today's marketplace.

The research focused on the population of administrators, managers, professional staff and above, that is those earning £20 000 or more per year. The findings are grouped under the topic headings set out below.

RETIREMENT AGE

The official retirement age in the companies surveyed was as shown in Figure 2.1. Officially the retirement age is 55–59 for 5 per cent of the companies, and 60 or over for 95 per cent of companies, with 40 per cent of companies allowing people to stay in their jobs until they are over the age of 65.

Over the past two years, however, the actual retirement age has been significantly lower, 50 per cent of people retiring between the ages of 55 and 59, and 50 per cent retiring between the ages of 60 and 64 (see Figure 2.2). The trend towards early retirement is very marked; previously research by Future Perfect revealed that the average age of retirement is currently around 57 for a significant proportion of large companies. This is particularly noticeable when compared with the forecast of the actual retirement age in five years' time (see Figure 2.3). This chart indicates that a considerable number of respondents are expecting little to change in 5 years; 52 per cent are forecast to retire between 60 and 64, compared with a stated actual of 50 per cent over the past two years. Yet the age of retirement has been falling steadily in recent years, is currently averaging 57, and is frequently occurring between ages 50 and 54.

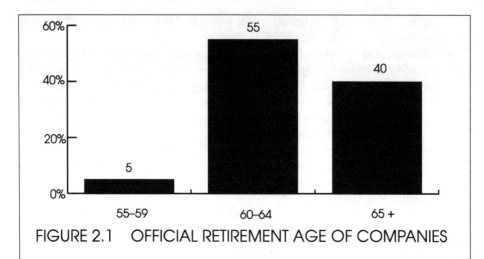

FIGURE 2.1   OFFICIAL RETIREMENT AGE OF COMPANIES

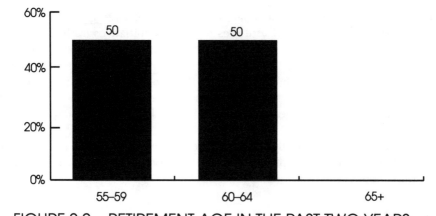

FIGURE 2.2   RETIREMENT AGE IN THE PAST TWO YEARS

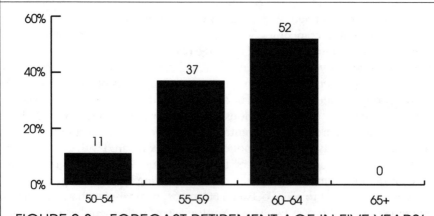

FIGURE 2.3   FORECAST RETIREMENT AGE IN FIVE YEARS'
TIME

It would appear, therefore, that there is a ten-year gap between current perceptions and the likely future retirement age. It is suggested that there will be very few who remain in their main careers between 60 and 64, and that a significant proportion will retire early between ages 50 and 54, shown as a forecast of only 11 per cent in Figure 2.3.

Retiring early however, need not imply a discontinuity in earning money or ending a working life. In fact, it need not involve retiring at all. Many people are becoming independent freelance agents or consultants and are taking advantage of the growing market for part-time mature staff, which reduces the costs for companies compared with using full-time employees. We see this practice of 'flexible resourcing' being a way forward for companies in the future, accounting for some 15 per cent of the workload in many instances. This brings into question whether we shall ever again see a stable state when 'normal' retirement conditions can be afforded.

EARLY RETIREMENT

The respondents were asked if their companies actively encouraged early retirement. Sixty two per cent said their companies did, although some claimed that this applied only during times of recession. The methods used varied from offering employees their pensions from the age of 55 with no actuarial reduction, to persuasive discussion in mid-career performance reviews, the offer of career counselling and a flexible use of pension schemes.

Pension arrangements play a large part in the early retirement package. Some companies have structured their schemes in such a way that after 15 years of pension contributions anyone can retire at 55 without actuarial reduction. Others offer cash incentives and supplementary payments to boost the employee's leaving package to what their pension would be at a given retirement age.

There appeared to be a ten-year span between companies for the minimum age a company considered it would be practicable or allowable for an employee to take early retirement (see Figure 2.4). Nearly 70 per cent of the organizations surveyed

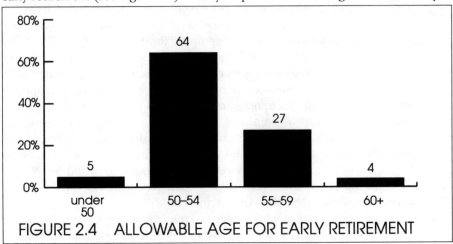

FIGURE 2.4   ALLOWABLE AGE FOR EARLY RETIREMENT

allow their employees to retire under the age of 55, and 96 per cent allow retirement before the employee reaches their 60th birthday; in practice the average age of retirement is 57 and falling.

Bearing in mind that we shall be running into shortages of younger employees in the labour force this under-utilization of older workers has some stark realities for industry and society. With organization structures moving towards the Shamrock organization described in Chapter 1, the core will be ever shrinking and the periphery ever evolving. There would appear to be a likely possibility of a future where a very significant number of people gain some organizational experience and then become freelancers, without ever reaching an age of retirement. This trend could herald the end of the company pension scheme, with personal pension plans becoming a much more relevant feature.

A concern of many middle managers facing early retirement has been not knowing what to do in the future, when so much of their personal identity and sense of self-worth has been bound up in their all-consuming occupational life. Some greatly fear the prospect of inactivity while they still have unexpired years of working life ahead of them. Yet employers seeking to encourage more early retirements have continued to improve the financial attractiveness of their packages to encourage a greater take-up of voluntary redundancy/early retirement, without appreciating until recently the fact that the issues for both the company and the employee are not principally financial but rather psychological and structural.

PHASED TRANSITION

There are many who genuinely want a change in their working pace and patterns before normal retirement age but who would be much happier with a gradual transition; there are some who want to start an activity on their own, but need a smooth transition and shy away from any sudden change that involves risk; and there are those who see their future in some form of consultancy, freelance or non-executive director work, the so called 'portfolio life', or 'going multiple' as the Americans call it.

What all these groups have in common is the need for what has become known as 'the decade of flexible retirement' or a planned transition. In fact retirement is an increasingly inappropriate word to reflect the needs of individuals and companies for meaningful endeavour in the second half or the third quarter of life. The Third Age can potentially be a very productive and fulfilling period, but it calls for very different planning and motivational approaches from those suited to the main career phases, and to which most companies' personnel philosophies and policies apply.

If organizations manage this transitional period well for their Third Age workforces, they can only win. Few companies, however, have yet to consider seriously the possibility of introducing some form of phased transition by which employees can retain strong, part-time working links with their firms after they technically retire. Future Perfect supports this concept strongly, because of the benefits to companies and individual employees alike if such arrangements can be put in place; some examples are described later in this book.

The low level of interest in applying a phased transition concept revealed by the study would appear to illustrate the inappropriateness of traditional management assumptions and responses to dealing with Third Age opportunities. It seems that companies are very apprehensive, partly due to the recession, and are lagging behind, unable to react fully to opportunities raised by the social, demographic and economic changes taking place.

PRE-RETIREMENT/MID-LIFE PLANNING

Ninety-five per cent of respondents said their companies provided pre-retirement courses for staff, although the time period in which they were undertaken varied considerably. Thirty-six per cent ran the courses in the year that the employee retired, 32 per cent did so the year before, and 32 per cent did so up to two years prior to retirement. However, in practice the actual time that this occurs is generally much closer to the retirement date than the responses might suggest, which mainly represent their intentions.

Over half the respondents claimed that mid-life planning was included in their course (61 per cent) while 39 per cent of courses did not consider this aspect. In our experience, the mid-life planning content tends to be a cursory review of future activities rather than exploring future opportunities in any depth, and we would therefore query the relatively high number which claim to fulfil this role in practice.

Rather than worrying about retirement itself, many Third Agers appear to concentrate on the job security and work satisfaction in the lead up to retirement, during their final years at work. The low level of interest in life planning is disturbing, but accurately reflects Future Perfect's experience over the last three years. Only a quarter were interested in early or systematic preparation for the mid-career life changes that affect us all, which is strangely and disturbingly at odds with the principle of training and retraining being espoused in official and corporate policy.

We consider that the mid-life planning process related to Third Age transition, i.e. from a main career to other chosen activities within a carefully constructed portfolio, should take at least one day and normally two days, with follow-up. Another issue is the extent to which the courses currently being operated are appropriate to today's climate of early retirement. The evidence suggests that most concentrate on genuine retirement and fail to provide the positive lead on 'portfolio careers' that would be desirable.

Revealingly organizations declared the low value attributed to the process of pre-retirement and mid-life planning. First, 45 per cent would not put a figure on it as some were doubtful they would pay at all, and no one was prepared to pay over £1 000. Otherwise, of those that did respond the figures were as shown in Figure 2.5. Only 40 per cent of the companies would be prepared to pay for a course in total, 25 per cent of the others would share the cost, and the remainder would be prepared only to provide information which the employees could take action on if they desired, at their own cost.

The current activity in this area cannot be construed as effective mid-life planning. It is more like giving swimming lessons to those on board the *Titanic* as it starts to sink! There is scope for a shift in investment priorities for training budgets and management development programmes. While it may seem that investing money in people leaving the company would be likely to yield a negative or zero

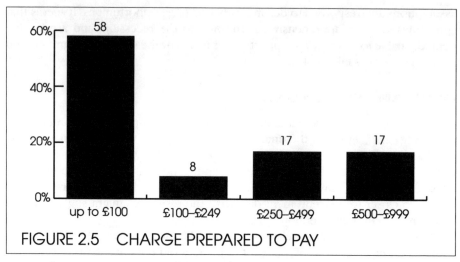

FIGURE 2.5   CHARGE PREPARED TO PAY

return, there is an opportunity for continuing part-time involvement in their future portfolio careers. It could therefore be short-sighted to cut off training and development support at a given age; the competence and potential contribution of an individual is a much more important factor. Companies should look at the likely implications of not training those people; without appropriate training and development people may not have the courage or know-how to pursue their career portfolios outside of the organization that would benefit the company (and the economy) in the future.

MEMBERSHIP NETWORK

Future Perfect considered plans to launch a membership network in the UK for people aged 45 plus. This could put them in touch with other people at a similar lifestage to allow an exchange of views, the formation of common-interest groups and the opportunity for people to promote themselves. Respondents were asked whether they would be prepared to support employees wishing to join this network and/or active pensioners likewise. The results are given in Figure 2.6. It is interesting that so many companies would be prepared to support a membership network as long as it did not cost them anything!

The network could incorporate a skills register for people who would be available for work in given fields. Thirty-six per cent of respondents said they would be likely to access the skills register to meet temporary resource needs, although few were prepared to comment on the amount that they would be prepared to pay, given that a specific requirement could be met. Only 4 per cent would be prepared to pay in excess of £250 for the service, while 18 per cent would pay between £100 and £249. Nine per cent would pay between £50 and £99, while only 5 per cent would pay up to £25. It is evident that a slick professional process would be necessary to enable such an operation to command a satisfactory response, using something like Dateline or other matching system, although whether this would be viable at £100 per successful appointment is questionable.

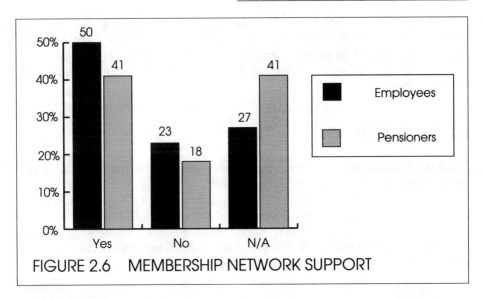

FIGURE 2.6   MEMBERSHIP NETWORK SUPPORT

IMPLICATIONS FOR COMPANIES

Downsizing is becoming commonplace during the recession, and companies may be gaining a false sense of security as many workers opt for early retirement. The current surplus of people can mask an underlying skills shortage which companies may have to fill with experienced over 40 year olds later on. Those companies with imagination who are prepared to adapt their policies to finance, train and develop people for the Third Age transition will be the ones to benefit.

Care needs to be taken in how to motivate and manage Third Age employees, so as to harness and apply their know-how and in some cases to prevent them from 'retiring at their desks'. If they are no longer interested in job advancement, then they perhaps need even more to be challenged and stimulated at the level they have reached, through involvement in company-wide projects or other initiatives which would provide appropriate variety and interest.

In the March 1992 joint IPM/Future Perfect conference on 'Human resource strategies for the Third Age' a number of speakers addressed the motivational and policy requirements of managing mature workforces. Retention and renewal factors for the over 40s were suggested and included a fair and competitive remuneration package, continuing challenge, continued investment in training and development, recognition of home-work priorities, finding the correct balance, and developing a culture in which promotion is not regarded as the sole criteria of success.

Managing rewards when no further promotion is possible needs to embrace traditional techniques of red-circling or personal grading. Alternatively, a basic salary progression can be turned into unconsolidated bonuses for continued competence performance, with one-off bonuses for specific achievement. Non-cash incentives can be used for the same purpose. 'Challenge elements' can be designed into the jobs, either through making them accountable for mentoring newer recruits or through assignments to lead or advise task forces and projects according to relevant experience. Third Age policy reviews and job studies undertaken by Future Perfect indicate that committee membership, for example, regarded as drudgery by some senior directors, may be seen as highly motivating and a basis for worthwhile contribution and creativity by talented, mid-career, mature managers.

SUMMARY FINDINGS

The research findings cover each particular issue in some detail. Ignoring the detail, however, how can we summarize the current views of organizations towards mature employees? There are a number of companies which have taken specific, positive action towards the encouragement of older workers, but this would seem to be the exception rather than the rule. Though it is not possible to generalize, we fear that the following statements might reflect the attitude of many UK companies:

> Older people are all right in their place, but give me younger, more energetic recruits to get the organization moving.

> Older employees are generally more expensive; we can get better value for money from those who are younger.

> We tend to find that older employees are generally less adaptable, though those with particular specialist capabilities are invaluable.

> Why should we be concerned about what employees do after they leave us through early retirement? They have their pension; beyond that it is not our responsibility.

These attitudes tend to change when voiced by executives in their mid-50s, however. Warning signals are beginning to emerge for him or her personally, and the viewpoint shifts quite dramatically. It is as though a wall of incomprehension is created between the corporate body and the individual, which is broken only when the individual concerned approaches the unmentionable stage himself or herself. Yet this time of transition may be one of the most significant events in the employee's life, and the reality of the situation is likely to make a very deep impression on each person. Organizations tend to be apprehensive about potential difficulties that may occur and frequently opt for a conventional pre-retirement course to salve their conscience. This may even be the case when the early retirement is sudden and unexpected.

Our observations are that the whole process is very much more complex and is not amenable to standard solutions; it can be very rewarding, though, if pursued with courage and imagination. This book explores potential solutions which are advantageous both to the company and the individual.

3

THE PROSPECT OF RETIREMENT

❖

In the 1960s and 1970s conventional career patterns consisted of a steady progression up the ladder until the age of retirement was reached (between 60 and 65), when the person concerned would leave his or her employment, beaming with joy, and would die a few years later. Leisure (and possibly DIY or gardening) appeared to be the main focus of life in retirement, as a reward for years of toil with the 'great reaper' ever present in the background.

Regrettably this attitude is still widespread today; people say 'oh well, of course, we are retired'. It implies withdrawal from active life at a point which is quite arbitrary, yet we have been conditioned to accept this negative stigma as part of our organizational lives. A former colleague mentioned recently 'they've called back Andrew Smith to carry out a job because they are so desperate; but he's retired. It's disgraceful'.

Yet the Third Age, approximately 50 to 75 or 80, is emerging as a new life phase, as a time of great opportunity for many. At the higher end people are becoming healthy and active for very much longer, as the statistics indicate, and at the lower end are leaving their main careers earlier. This trend is particularly marked during a recessionary climate, in which companies have used early retirement as a prominent device for culling staff numbers. There is thus a period of some 15 to 25 years after retirement for people to develop new skills, choose new activities, start new careers (paid or unpaid). As yet this progressive attitude tends to be the exception, and many people are rooted in the traditional concept of a retired existence.

As the age of retirement descends further (frequently to the early 50s when pension rules allow for retiring early) conventional views will cease to be acceptable. Gradually it will become the norm, we believe, for individuals to develop a new lifestyle and career pattern for their Third Age, as indicated earlier.

SELF-ESTEEM COMES FROM A PROPER JOB

The Times leader on 24 September 1993 gave some hope that a public debate is starting. It reported a British Psychological Society Conference paper which showed that what most people regard as fulfilment can only be achieved in paid work – the subtitle was 'Having a job seems to be necessary for self-esteem'.

'In other words no matter how worthwhile or energetic a leisure pastime may be, it cannot impart the same sense of purpose and self-respect as a "proper" job' – a subtle psychological difference between working for a livelihood and even the most assiduous hobby. What is suggested by the responses of those who filled in Dr Haworth's (the researcher's) questionnaires is that the very constraints of working life are what make it satisfying. The findings refer to factors like 'time structure, social contact, collective purpose, social identity or status and regular activity' – having to be at a given place at a particular time with actual deadlines for completing tasks, working towards some larger goal with a team of people in which everyone has a specified role and having all of this take place in some customary, habitual way.

Being compelled to take part by some force outside personal whim – extrinsic motivation, as opposed to intrinsic – seems to be the key factor in making paid work a more valuable source of psychological well-being. Having objectives and structures imposed by others lends credibility to an enterprise. In leisure activities, even ones that are socially useful, the freedom to create personal goals and time limits often degenerates into an open-ended activity in which people find it difficult to maintain a sense of purpose.

People often mentioned that being at work involved doing things that were initially disliked. The overcoming of their own resistance to do the task gave a form of gratification that was particularly difficult to match outside the workplace. Paid work now seems to be taken as the measure of successful adulthood in a way that it would not have been a century ago, when whole classes of society did not expect to work for a living. The fact that virtually all unpaid activity is now regarded as leisure, and by connotation unserious, shows how much the idea of employment (paid work) dominates modern life.

Unemployed people (with the theme 'there is nothing like work to keep you satisfied' in mind) often try to obtain the same sense of satisfaction by working hard at their leisure activities, but without complete success. The trouble with leisure, Dr Haworth found, is that there is no supervisor forcing you to do things that you would rather avoid. Overcoming a reluctance to carry out tasks that were unpleasant gave much satisfaction. These studies are based on Professor Marie Jahoda's theory that, apart from the financial rewards, work promotes happiness by providing workers with a time structure, social contacts, a collective purpose, a sense of identity and more regular activity. Among managers a sense of collective purpose and status would appear to be the most important routes to achieving self-esteem.

PERSONALITIES AT WORK

How do employees aged 45 plus see their future lives at the present time? Based on countless personal interviews and counselling sessions we illustrate the personal feelings involved by ascribing them to typical characters:

O   *The supreme optimist:* I am 53 and am looking for two promotions before I retire at 60. The company has not taken full advantage of my talents so far, and I feel that I have got at least two more jobs in me before I go. I would hate retirement, anyway, and I shall demonstrate my loyalty to the company by staying on as long as I can.

O   *The rebel:* I am longing for the day when the company will agree to my retiring early. I cannot stand the responsibility, the difficulties, the relentless pace of work and rate of change. I would like to be independent rather than be at the beck and call of others. I have all sorts of ideas about the future; just let it happen soon.

O   *The hero:* I shall retire early when the company considers it appropriate. No doubt they will treat me fairly over this. My qualities are such that I should have little difficulty in finding another job or a selection of jobs. Mind you, I shall miss my work colleagues and all the facilities available at the plant. I shall have to make sure that these standards are maintained in my new jobs. Perhaps it won't be quite so easy after all.

O   *The hard worker:* When I retire I am never going to work again. I reckon I deserve it. I can afford to go to the pub for lunch every day, and Muriel and I will do just what we please. A bit of gardening, the occasional game of tennis, and visiting the family will suit us fine. I have done my bit. It's a mug's game to try anything else at my age.

O   *The worrier:* I'm scared stiff of retirement. It's like a black hole opening up in front of me. I am trying to stay on as long as possible to avoid having to face it. What will I do with my time? I shall be a nobody. I shall be cut off from colleagues and all the things I enjoy in my work. What on earth can I do about it? It seems like the end.

O   *The opportunist:* I hear that they are offering voluntary early retirement on favourable terms. Perhaps I could at last start up that antiques/paintings studio I have been dreaming about. The children have left home, the mortgage is paid off and my husband would probably like to make it a joint venture, as he is retiring soon. I'll find out more.

These characters encompass the main comments and feelings that we have observed. It is difficult, however, to describe such a range of personal feelings and situations with the clarity and depth they deserve. There are some important common strands which run through the different attitudes expressed, which we believe are worth noting; these can be described under the headings of Third Age values and fear of retirement.

THIRD AGE VALUES

It is fascinating how people's values can change as they approach their 50s. Some interesting research has been carried out by Taylor Nelson and Applied Futures which is referred to in Francis Kinsman's *Millennium 2000*, W H Allen, 1990. The research plots the characteristics of people in society at different life stages. It divides the population into seven categories, which, for simplicity, can be grouped into three main types of people:

O   *Sustenance-driven*, who are disproportionately concerned with security, with surviving physically and maintaining a comfortable position in life. They are generally inclined towards living a conservative, clannish, narrow type of existence, and tend to resist change.

O   *Outer-directed*, whose motivation is the search for esteem and status. They judge themselves by the way they believe others see them. They want to live with or marry the right person, to have the right job, to live in the right area, to drive the right car and to send their children to the right schools. They aim at social and financial improvement through conspicuous achievement and consumption. They tend to be educated, intelligent and supporters of the *status quo*.

O   *Inner-directed*, whose dominant motivation is self-actualization or fulfilment. They are largely unconcerned by the opinions of the world at large, since the criteria for success lie within them. They usually have a wide range of interests, a sound grasp of current events and a high tolerance of other people's activities. Their values, opinions and beliefs are based more on personal growth, freedom of expression, quality of life and so on. Money tends to represent the means of doing things that interest them rather than being an indicator of success.

An interesting feature demonstrated by this research is that a significant proportion of people change category as they get older. The move into the Third Age can coincide with a state sometimes referred to as the mid-life crisis, when individuals call their values into question and make a reassessment of priorities. The research shows that inner-directed values are appealing to an increasing number of people, of whom many are Third Agers. Inner-directeds accounted for as much as 36 per cent of the population in 1987.

Employees frequently start to recognize that there could be greater satisfactions in their career than continuing in a role which is beginning to lose its sparkle. 'There must be more to life' is a phrase which occurs time and again, which argues well for a reappraisal and development of new plans.

FEAR OF RETIREMENT

We have found that the degree of apprehension normally varies directly with the length of service in a given organization or role, such as in public service or a large industrial company, which is normally a career life. It is hardly surprising, considering the hours that most of us work in our main career, that we should be fearful of an unknown future lifestyle, which may well be quite different to the routines that are so ingrained and familiar to us. It is, in effect, the start of a bereavement process, in which the losses are real, deep and personal. The fears, we suggest, include a perceived loss of the following:

○   *Status*, since one can change, at a stroke, from a person with a title and organizational role to become an individual who exists just as himself or herself, with no recognized standing in society apart from being a pensioner. 'What shall I put on my visiting card?' cried one person at a Future Perfect forum.

○   *Life support system*, which incorporates all the physical trappings of office or factory life, including free heat, light, accommodation and possibly a canteen, a secretary or a car. These benefits are frequently taken for granted.

○   *Administrative facilities*, such as the use of a telephone, fax, photocopier which are tended to be regarded as an integral part of normal life. There is also the administration of pay, personal tax and National Insurance, with readily accessible research information available on a variety of relevant topics in one's field.

○   *Money*, which would normally represent a considerable reduction in the current level of earnings. Though a pension and other investment income may be entirely adequate, there can be a feeling that money is equivalent to personal value or recognition. Expressed as 'I am going to be poor', this can represent a very strong concern and is possibly evidence of low self-esteem. Frequently, though, the lack of a reasonable income can be a real problem and active consideration needs to be given to supplementing an inadequate pension or poor severance payments.

○   *Colleagues*, where the potential loss of work friends whom one has known and respected for many years is a very significant factor. Whatever a person does next, there is undoubtedly a separation from the current work 'family', and for many people this can be the most serious and painful loss.

○   *Rejection*, which is felt to varying degrees depending on circumstances. If early retirement has been instigated by the company, rather than by the individual, there can be deep resentment and a sense of affront. The suddenness with which this frequently occurs can exacerbate this feeling to a distressing degree.

○   *Life partnership*, the format for which has been based on set work routines developed over decades. Both partners normally find that the projected, uncertain lifestyle patterns implicit in retirement can be a fearful prospect (possibly even despite a declared delight in being able to spend more time together).

○   *Lifestyles and the use of time*, for which no future pattern yet exists. The extent to which it might be possible to work, paid or unpaid, or choose other fulfilling activities, is frequently delayed for the future, and can be a frightening prospect if not properly addressed (the 'black hole').

○   *Mortality*, since many identify retirement as the phase immediately prior to dependency, decline and death. Being reminded that one is mortal can add to the fears described above. Good health is often quoted by Third Agers as being their most important objective in their new life phase.

From our observations we believe that everyone, even the most successful executives, suffer to a greater or lesser extent from many of these anxieties. It is healthy and necessary, however, to recognize their existence so that the concerns can be appropriately addressed. We would go further and claim that the whole process of such an important transition, or 'passage' as the researcher Gail Sheehy calls it, should be explored further. In her book *Pathfinders* she describes 'the anatomy of a passage', and identifies the qualities she has discovered in a typical person that has successfully made such a transition.

4

INDIVIDUALS AND THE THIRD AGE

❖

F actual information about ways in which people view the prospect of the Third Age, particularly when they retire, is scant. There are some theories and models as mentioned earlier, but to our knowledge, little, if any, research has been carried out on the views and opinions of mature people who are still in their main career and are approaching a transition in their 50s or early 60s. Future Perfect therefore commissioned the British Market Research Bureau to carry out a survey on 'Attitudes to the Third Age' involving some 220 interviews in March 1992.

It is important at the outset to note that people do not appear to think much about retirement or Third Age living until it is upon them. One personnel director confessed that he had felt quite threatened and frightened by a meeting to discuss Third Age transition just one year before he retired; he then started giving some thought to the implications for himself. He had forced the topic to remain right at the back of his mind and was denying his fear of taking this, for him, fateful step. Consequently he viewed the prospect of retirement with dread, so much so that he felt unable to take advantage of the transition support offered to him, because he had barely acknowledged that this change was happening, and that it could perhaps be positive.

The short time window when people do think about retirement or the Third Age, has a considerable bearing on the research findings. One has to appreciate that the bulk of the respondents will not have been in that time window, and will have provided views from their own position of non-involvement at the present time. The responses therefore require careful consideration, in that they will mostly represent immediate responses rather than considered views.

The importance of this 'time window' factor is evident when one sees the trauma that sudden, unexpected early retirement brings to many people. We have recently been counselling a successful executive who had just been moved by his firm to a new location and was then asked to retire six months later. Aged 58 (when it could be argued that he should already have been thinking about this prospect), he was completely disoriented by the event. He had been a consistent achiever, looking to achieve greater things each day, and was the proud possessor of an expensive home with a happy family. He, too, had not acknowledged that his main career would end at some stage, and that he had a few questions he would have to ask himself. After a fallow period he began to make decisions about the course his life would take so that he would again, on his own initiative, be an achiever in very different fields.

These two examples illustrate the potential psychological difficulties that can be experienced if Third Age transition is handled badly, either by an employer or by an individual, or indeed not handled at all. Retirement seems to be almost a taboo topic in business circles, rather like death or serious illness, though attitudes are changing as more and more individuals develop their own successful portfolio careers.

IMPORTANCE OF LIFE FEATURES

Respondents were asked to rank five life features in terms of their importance to them at this stage in their lives. The proportion ranking each of the life features as being the most important is shown in Figure 4.1.

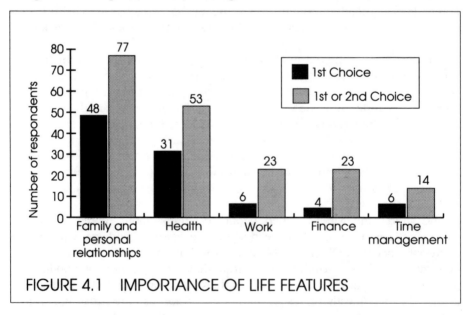

FIGURE 4.1   IMPORTANCE OF LIFE FEATURES

Are there any surprises here? The chart shows a very marked contrast between the first two features and the rest. The extent of the differences is perhaps unexpected, and even more so the way that health appears very prominently in second place. It is hardly surprising that people would generally rate family and personal relationships as a key to their lives, but one might expect health to be more equal with the rest unless there had been a history of ill health, either personally or in the family. Work and finance come low down the scale in importance terms; these features will all now be examined further.

FAMILY AND PERSONAL RELATIONSHIPS

The vast majority of the sample (85 per cent) were either married or living as if married. These people were asked how, following retirement, they expected their relationship to be affected. Figure 4.2 shows their answers.

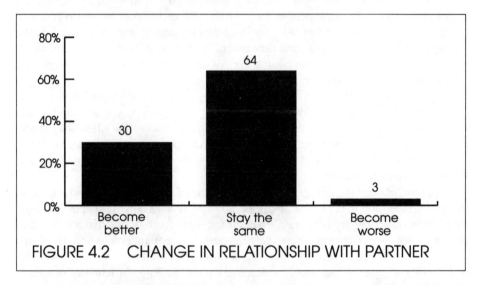

FIGURE 4.2   CHANGE IN RELATIONSHIP WITH PARTNER

This is an optimistic view of the future! We have known many cases where the period of adjustment following retirement has been fraught, requiring substantial compromise in the life patterns of the partners. However, it is encouraging that such an optimistic outlook is put forward, but we fear that it is somewhat a 'blue sky' approach and possibly unrealistic. We find in our workshops, when couples are drawing up their life plans, that unknown or unacknowledged desires emerge and a considerable amount of negotiation has to take place. It is only when the change is firmly on the horizon that discussions occur and potential difficulties are appreciated. Most people seem to have a simple image of retirement, frequently one of contentment at not having to work.

In the light of these findings, it is important to consider that every relationship is tested when a significant change in life patterns occurs, and this can represent a critical stage in the relationship. Some partners have led very separate lives, particularly the high-powered executive whose wife has had to subordinate her wishes to accommodate the inconvenient demands of her husband. We have known couples on our workshops where the wife regards herself as a non-person, with no qualities of her own other than looking after her husband. One such wife had to be ready to deal with her husband at any hour to meet whatever need, because of the nature of his job. The most hopeful signs are demonstrated when a wife has had a career of her own, when it becomes more natural for the two lifestyle patterns to dovetail together, and in such circumstances a positive transition to the Third Age appears to be achieved much more easily. There can be instances, however, where the wife has been so successful at this task that she becomes the active partner and the husband finds himself in a subsidiary, home-based role. This role reversal can be exceptionally hard for some people to adapt to, which can explain why counselling agencies find that many couples seek help in later life.

Yet our sample, still in the enthusiasm of a pre-retirement existence, assume that their relationship will prosper as they cross the barrier into the Third Age. It is possible for this to be so, if people intend to be somewhat passive in this phase of their lives, but for those who are active and determined to live life to the full, the change will be anything but straightforward. It is, in effect, similar to the initial stages of the Second Age, when people in their teens or early twenties start on their main career and begin to create a family.

We would contend, therefore, that people generally are unprepared for life in the Third Age. The sample were also asked whether they would be interested in some form of counselling to enrich their personal relationships when they retire. The response was overwhelmingly negative, with 92 per cent being firmly not interested and only 5 per cent claiming to be fairly interested. This shows the gap between needs and wants.

The main obstacle to participating in some form of involvement would appear to be the conventional British 'stiff upper lip' and fear of anything that is faintly psychological. Yet there is generally a need for some form of positive intervention at critical stages in our lives; marriage preparation or enhancement and Third Age planning possibly represent the most significant opportunities in this context. With regard to marriage, for example, the Association for Marriage Enrichment run some excellent workshops, which, despite being directly relevant to a high proportion of marriages, are only few in number each year, in response to a relatively low level of demand.

The lack of openness in dealing with oneself and one's partner seems to be an overriding problem for the current generation; the façade obscures the reality. Perhaps such reticence will fade as time passes, and our children and grandchildren will demonstrate and accept more genuine views on such important issues.

HEALTH

All the participants were asked about their current state of health and were given the opportunity of assessing it as one of four conditions as indicated in Figure 4.3. Given the British tendency to understatement, we suppose that 62 per cent believed that they were satisfactory and 37 per cent are less sure about their medical condition. Perhaps of more interest is the incidence of medical health checks

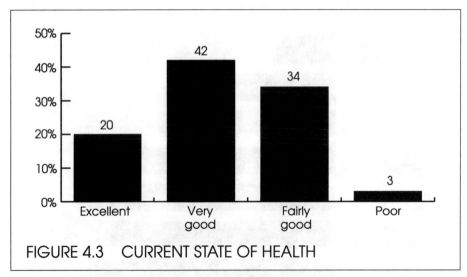

FIGURE 4.3   CURRENT STATE OF HEALTH

carried out. Seventy-three per cent of the sample had undergone medical checks while 26 per cent had not. Of those that had a medical health check 27 per cent had taken place within the last year, 17 per cent 1–2 years ago, 12 per cent 3–4 years ago and the remaining 17 per cent over 4 years ago.

From an occupational health point of view, these findings are somewhat disappointing. Surely preventive medicine is concerned with assessing conditions well in advance of any necessary treatment. The older you get the more prone you are to life-threatening ailments. Organizations are often prepared to pay for regular medical checks for their senior employees, but what about the needs of the remainder, and the period of time after which they have all retired? Employers may no longer be directly interested in their health, but it would be encouraging if, as part of their benefits packages, they could do more in this direction, linked to their pension or severance arrangements.

We also asked the participants if they would be interested in having a medical check now. Only 34 per cent would be, if they could afford it. The relevant providers would do well to address this need. An interesting slant on this finding is that there is a significant difference between those who wish to work after retirement (40 per cent of those wanting a health check) compared with those who do not (only 25 per cent). This reinforces the point that many people only value themselves in relationship to work. Their health is surely just as important regardless of their lifestyle, but the findings conclude otherwise. Even 39 per cent of those who have *never* had a health check are interested in having one now, so this is firmly on the agenda for Third Agers.

WORK

There was an interesting response to the questions relating to work, which does not appear to rank highly in the overall selection. When asked about certain

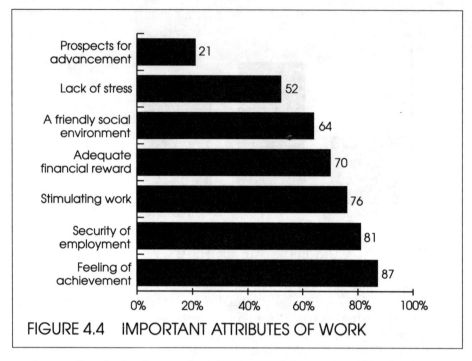

FIGURE 4.4   IMPORTANT ATTRIBUTES OF WORK

attributes of work, the features listed in Figure 4.4 were considered to be either extremely or very important.

It is hardly surprising that people in this age group should rate prospects for advancement low, in that promotion frequently ceases to be a reality by the time an employee reaches the age of 50, if not 45 in many organizations. However, the bulk of the rankings appear to be at odds with the experience of people who have already retired. What many Third Agers welcome is the lack of stress in their new portfolio careers (compared with their main career, where it is normally high) and miss more than anything else the friendly social environment of being among colleagues who are always there. These two factors (at 52 per cent and 64 per cent) are rated low in comparison with the conventional responses of worthwhile achievement, security of employment, stimulating work and adequate financial reward. These rather more obvious features, which are rated so highly, are however unlikely to be maintained in the Third Age unless exceptional action is taken by the individual himself or herself.

The implication of the research is that the individual expects his or her employer to deal with all these aspects, which is why security of employment becomes such a prominent feature, for which most of the respondents will be entirely dependent on their employer (who can no longer fulfil earlier expectations). This suggests that the responses, quite naturally, relate as much to Second Age desires as to the Third Age situation, when views invariably change. In our experience, the quest for worthwhile achievement persists well into the Third Age, and it is this prominent desire which we believe should be encouraged and exploited to the full.

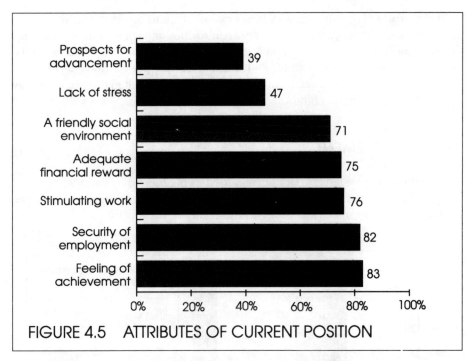

FIGURE 4.5   ATTRIBUTES OF CURRENT POSITION

As a comparison with the perceived rankings of importance, the respondents also rated the features in their current situation in a similar way (see Figure 4.5). These rankings link directly with the perceived level of importance expressed earlier, which is hardly surprising, though the prospects for advancement appear to merit a much higher satisfaction level (39 per cent instead of 21 per cent) thus perhaps demonstrating an over-optimistic view of immediate career development prospects.

In several of our studies we have met fairly typical managers who have felt that they had at least one promotional step in front of them, yet they are candidates for early retirement. If only organizations could help to establish more direct communications about future career prospects, a sense of realism rather than fantasy, a great deal of unnecessary distress could be prevented. One interviewee confessed that he was overjoyed when an application for the next year's season ticket loan was approved; it meant that his immediate future was assured. Should employees have to ascertain their future career in this way?

TIME MANAGEMENT

The authors of this book have great difficulty in managing their own time, and hence feel very vulnerable in discussing this issue; everyone else is sure to manage their time better! It is something that most of us struggle with in our main career, with a prospect of improvement in the second (though the authors are doubtful of the fulfilment of this projection).

The majority of the interviewees (85 per cent) claim to be satisfied with the way in which their time is currently split between various activities. More than a third (35 per cent) are very satisfied. This is perhaps surprising, and may indicate a relatively low accommodation with life and work. Most busy people find it a continual struggle to get the balance right, and the complacency implicit in the response may demonstrate that certain compromises have been achieved.

AGE OF RETIREMENT

We asked the respondents what they regarded as the 'normal retirement age' and also at what age they intended to retire. The responses were very revealing (see Figure 4.6) and are in stark contrast to the reality of the situation. Other surveys

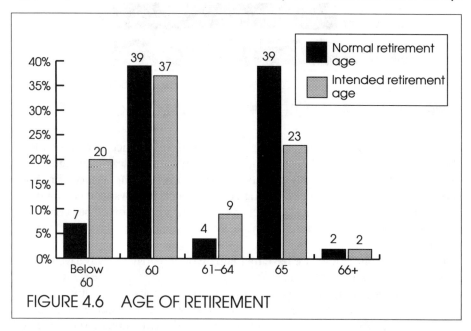

FIGURE 4.6   AGE OF RETIREMENT

indicate that the average age of retirement is now around 57, yet only 20 per cent would appear to recognize this fact, whilst 37 per cent indicate their intention to retire at age 60. What about the 34 per cent who intend to retire beyond age 60 though? We suggest that this is quite unrealistic. The sooner people start to plan in mid-life, well before they move on from their main career in their 50s, the more likely they are to achieve a satisfying Third Age.

FINANCE

The sample appeared to see finance in some kind of entire life perspective. When we asked them how adequate their current financial situation was, and what

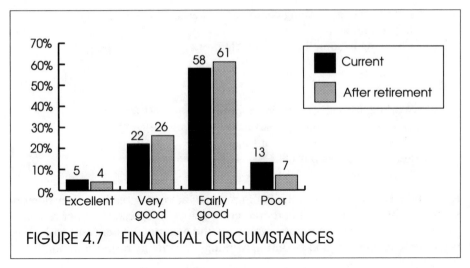

FIGURE 4.7   FINANCIAL CIRCUMSTANCES

their situation would be likely to be after retirement the response was as shown in Figure 4.7.

All respondents were asked whether they had ever had a professional review of their financial arrangements. Forty-nine per cent had done so (29 per cent within the last year) while 51 per cent had not a review of any kind. This is surprising, as many people seem to live from month to month, ensuring that they are able to meet continuing commitments. Retirement, though, can make a significant difference to earnings levels and one might expect that a review would be welcomed at this critical juncture. Not so, however, according to our research. The level of interest in having a review was 12 per cent interested, 17 per cent not very interested and 71 per cent not at all interested. This we also find surprising.

There is an undoubted need for professional assistance with an individual's financial affairs, and participants in Future Perfect workshops consider it a priority. Note the caution here, compared with the level of interest expressed for a medical health check, in which 34 per cent were interested.

ATTITUDES TO RETIREMENT

Over half the respondents intended to work following their retirement from their main career. Twenty-four per cent intended to take paid work and 35 per cent wanted to do voluntary work. Eleven per cent of the sample wanted to do both paid and voluntary work. Thirty-two per cent had decided that once they retired that was that, enough was enough and they were not going to work again, while 16 per cent were undecided on the matter. Only 5 per cent of those intending to work expected to work full time; 86 per cent looked to part-time employment to fulfil their needs.

As the type of work they would go for, the following inclinations emerged:

Changing to something completely different	47%
In present field	25%
Changing to something slightly different	15%
Don't know	13%

and

Working for a charity or the community	71%
One or more businesses part time	25%
Operating as a freelance consultant	15%
Setting up a new business	7%
Don't know	11%

Again there is an overlap, but the findings make interesting reading. They demonstrate that the wish to work after retirement is quite widespread, at 48 per cent, and that there is a range of intentions expressed, the majority (62 per cent) wishing to do something different and favouring working for a charity or the community (71 per cent)

However, how realistic are these aspirations? Expressed at some distance from retirement they sound plausible, but the moment of truth comes when they have to be put into practice. Ford carried out some interesting research with retirers about three years ago, comparing intentions before retiring with the actual situation one year later. This has revealed a significant shortfall between intentions to work and subsequent success in achieving that situation.

PLANNING FOR RETIREMENT

We asked the respondents whether or not they had planned their retirement activities. The response is shown in Figure 4.8. These findings do not accord with our experience. We can only suppose that 'fairly planned' implies that some general

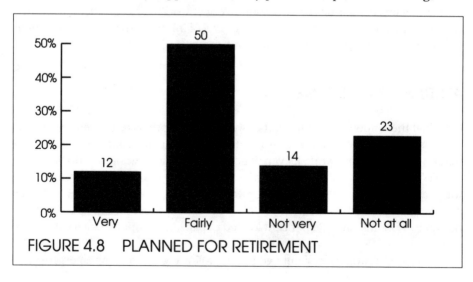

FIGURE 4.8   PLANNED FOR RETIREMENT

thoughts about the future were held, e.g. 'I'll take a part-time job, play golf and spend more time gardening', rather than a substantive plan drawn up.

Our experience shows that, when the retirement date becomes imminent, there is often a long period of inaction while the person adjusts to the reality of the situation. There was one lady on one of our workshops who could only write down the date she was leaving the company on her planning sheet; she could not bring herself to think through the implications in practical terms.

We also asked the sample how interested they were in receiving assistance with life planning prior to retirement. Only 22 per cent were interested. Our researchers told us that people appeared to be unfamiliar with the term 'life planning', and that this could be a significant reason for the low response. However, it also illustrates that people try to avoid thinking about their retirement until as late as possible, in some cases, the day after the retirement party.

PERSONAL ATTITUDES

We wanted to test people's attitudes to retirement so we asked them whether they agreed or disagreed with some statements that we drew up according to our experiences in workshops. The results are interesting:

	Agree (%)	Disagree (%)
I see retirement as an opportunity to relax and do what I want.	89	7
I see retirement as an opportunity to do something useful in my life.	59	32
I would welcome the opportunity for early retirement.	57	36
I am looking forward to moving on from my current career.	32	59
I am worried about what I will do when I retire.	9	90

A significant proportion of the respondents welcome early retirement, but at the same time are apprehensive about leaving their current career. This dichotomy is quite understandable, though, and it reveals the difficulty of 'positive early retirement' gaining acceptance as a normal hypothesis. People often find it difficult to be honest with themselves early enough; these particular findings tend to indicate some acknowledgement of the issues involved.

AGE DISCRIMINATION

Most of us believe that age discrimination exists, particularly with regard to employment, but it does not normally affect us unless we are old ourselves. Again we put statements to the sample and asked them whether they agreed with them or not:

	Agree (%)	Disagree (%)
The older you get the harder it is to get a job.	88	7
I believe a new government should introduce legislation to prevent discrimination against older people when they are applying for jobs.	66	25
Society's attitude towards the over 40s is changing for the better.	48	32

The appeal for legislation from 66 per cent of the sample is significant. Though we ourselves are unconvinced that legislation is necessarily the answer on policy grounds, this seems to represent the strength of feeling on this topic. Attitudes surely have to change on this front, and the positive qualities of mature workers become recognized and valued.

Market and demographic forces, that is the potential shortage of younger people as the economy eventually recovers, are likely to do as much to change things as anything. Look at the initiatives taken by the retail chains such as B&Q and Tesco. They have been delighted with their experiments in recruiting mature workers, and it is now part of their culture. We would place emphasis on the growing use of mature people as subcontractors for given services or projects as the optimum way for the future. Whether or not legislation would assist is a moot point.

We would like to see people assessed on the basis of competence regardless of age. One or two companies in our survey observed this practice and the outcome is impressive. Needless to say, however, such organizations have suffered considerable purges before they reached a point where most posts were solely competence based.

EMPLOYER'S VIEWS

	Agree (%)	Disagree (%)
My company does a lot to help employees prepare for retirement.	38	44
My employer is becoming more negative towards me personally as I move towards retirement.	9	90
My employer would be likely to contribute to life-planning services.	24	59

The above list demonstrates a number of features. It suggests that mature employees see themselves as being still very much in the fold, and are comfortable with the way that their firm regards them. This view can change, however, as early retirement beckons or is imposed, and the responses show a distinct proportion who will be unlikely to gain support from their employer in this transition.

The 44 per cent and 59 per cent responses to the first and last statements are not encouraging, and they appear consistent with the findings from other research carried out. One large employer now restricts assistance to the provision of a retirement handbook (because previous pre-retirement events had turned into inappropriate jamborees) and other employers either do nothing or provide a useful short course geared to genuine retirement or withdrawal. We believe that the needs of individuals are scarcely being met, and who better, partially in their own interests, than the employer to take the lead here. Such practice is evidently beneficial in human resources policy terms; let us hope that progressive improvements will be introduced in this important field.

CONCLUSIONS

The research reviewed in this chapter points to a number of conclusions:

O   There is a significant lack of awareness of the Third Age and its implications and opportunities. Many of the responses appear to reflect Second Age views that are not yet broadened to embrace the Third Age perspective. This time window factor, where the span of awareness is currently very limited, is an important feature here.

O   Untapped potential is ready and waiting, but requires empowering. The population appears to divide itself currently between those who see retirement as withdrawal, and the growing remainder who believe that there may be exciting possibilities for their future lives.

O   Only partly formed, imprecise views are in place at this stage. Moving on from one's main career after considerable years of service can be a traumatic experience and merits greater attention.

O   Hence transition support is necessary to enable people to come to terms with their future state, and be able to plan their lives accordingly. Employers are best placed to provide a framework for this support, which can benefit all the parties.

O   It is an important issue for the UK as the number of younger people declines and healthy and active Third Agers become available to make a contribution to the economy. Their active independence should be fostered and harvested. This growing section of the population is probably the most under-utilized resource in the country. It is time that their benefit and worth are appreciated and tapped for the welfare of the individuals, companies and the economy as a whole.

5

A FRAMEWORK FOR POLICY

❖

C onsider an average company which, in recent years, has had its share of retirements (some a little early, mutually agreed), with redundancies in particular areas. This practice appears to have created few ripples of discontent within the organization (apart from the people directly affected), and the commercial advantages of slimming down in this way are self-evident.

WHY HAVE A POLICY?

Why should a company need to consider developing a specific policy for the management and motivation of mature employees, therefore? It is vitally important that this question should be considered fairly and squarely before discussing the possible ingredients of a policy. The reasons, which together we believe to be very compelling, include the following.

COMMERCIAL

o   The competitive environment involves a relentless pressure on costs, of which staffing costs normally form a very significant proportion. If a company continues to shed mature, experienced employees at a significant rate it will reach a point at which it is in serious danger of damaging its core capability. We know of companies that have gone beyond this point and regretted it.

o   Mature employees represent a valuable asset through the skills, experience and commitment which they bring to the tasks they carry out. Such a resource requires managing and motivating in a particular way if full benefit is to be gained from those qualities.

o   An inevitable pattern for the future will be a greater use of flexible resourcing, with people working on a part-time, project or seasonal basis. Mature employees could be in the vanguard of this movement. This presents a remarkable opportunity for a creative, commercial approach to be adopted.

O   As the economy recovers, there will be a shortage of qualified younger people. Appropriate mechanisms will need to be in place for optimizing the use of older people.

MOTIVATIONAL

O   The effect on younger staff of releasing a significant number of older staff can be seriously negative, if handled badly. We know of many instances where sudden, enforced retirements have had a very harmful impact on those that have remained. The danger here is that instability is created, performance declines and people are prone to leave when the opportunity arises.

O   The older people themselves frequently feel demotivated and threatened if no clear policy exists. At the same time, they have a changing set of life and career values, which scarcely appear to be recognized by employers. If their motivation is enhanced, their performance will improve.

O   The whole transition process itself is a specific feature, with strong motivational implications, as described at some length earlier.

SOCIAL

O   Ageism is becoming recognized as a missing ingredient from Equal Opportunities policy and practice. Companies promoting excellence will inevitably wish to create and adopt a sound policy in this context.

O   The Carnegie Inquiry identifies the trend towards an ageing population, with a progressively increasing proportion of mature people becoming economically inactive. The country can ill afford the high level of support costs involved; in terms of social responsibility, therefore, anything that companies can do to help employees achieve a productive Third Age would be beneficial.

Together these commercial, motivational and social factors provide a powerful justification for developing a policy framework for managing and motivating mature employees, we believe. Any company which claims to operate on a total quality management basis cannot afford to neglect the various factors we have set out above.

POLICY DEVELOPMENT

REVIEW

How should a company develop such a policy? In our experience the process needs to start with a deep awareness of the issues, and this would normally be achieved through an investigative review directed specifically at Third Age issues. The process would normally involve interviewing some 20 to 50 employees aged 40 plus, depending on the size of the organization, on an individual, face-to-face arrangement. It can also be helpful to bring small groups of recently retired employees together to obtain their views on particular aspects, such as the transition process. The topics covered by the review would generally include the following.

Business priorities, and their implications for human resource planning

O   management of change
O   cost effectiveness
O   new organizational formats
O   company age and length of service profiles

Impact on mature employees

O   attitudes perceived
O   fear of uncertainty

Career development

O   career management/succession planning
O   training and development
O   career prospects

Third Age Transition

O   the transition process
O   transition support
O   pension implications

Each interviewee responds on two counts, on the one hand representing the company in a managerial or professional capacity and on the other speaking as an individual employee. In this way a great deal is revealed about the organization, its culture, its practices and some specific insights into the personal plans and intentions of older people. From this wealth of material it is possible to make a penetrating analysis of the company regarding Third Age issues. Once that has been done the formulation of a policy that addresses each of the main features identified by the review may commence.

POLICY ELEMENTS

The policy that will be developed through this process will vary in relation to the detailed findings and the company's existing employment policies. In essence, however, it would be likely to cover the following areas, for which we set out a suggested optimum.

Recruitment

Following the IPM guidelines (see Appendix II), age will not be a prejudicial factor in recruitment practice, and no age requirements will be specified in advertisements unless there are exceptional reasons, such as demanding physical tasks.

Career development

The company practices lifelong skills training, and self-development programmes are in place for implementation by employees of all ages. The company operates an annual performance and appraisal and feed-back procedure, which incorporates discussion and agreement on personal targets regarding performance and development in the coming year. Promotion and other appointments are based strictly on an assessment of competence rather than age or length of service. Age is regarded as an unimportant factor in career terms, whereas capability and achievement of targets are the main determinants for compensation and promotion.

Special career reviews are held at age 40 to 50 to examine how employees can best progress towards a satisfactory Third Age transition. Redeployment opportunities exist for mature employees who may wish to make an internal transfer as part of their transition plans.

Flexible resourcing

The company plans to cover 20 per cent of its future workload through a flexible resourcing programme, employing people on a part-time, project or seasonal basis. Employees will normally have the opportunity of transferring to work on this basis as they see fit, either during the course of their main career or through early retirement. In appropriate circumstances the company will offer them continuing work amounting to between 45 and 60 days a year for 1 or 2 years after formally leaving the company. Personal financial planning assistance is available through the company's brokers to deal with the financial implications of the transition, in addition to the company's pensions information service regarding their own pension details.

Continuing support

The company operates an employee assistance programme, whereby any employee can 'phone directly to receive counselling assistance with life and career issues. This help will naturally be available to mature employees at the time of Third Age transition.

In our view, the policy should be such that, once implemented and absorbed into the organization, a typical mature employee should be able to say:

I realize that I am getting older and that, one day soon, I shall move on to other things. The company is flexible and understanding about this, and will help me to decide when I should technically retire (which I realize is likely to occur before normal retirement age). I feel valued for what I do at present, and appreciate the fact that the company is helping me to plan my future career, both for my remaining years within the organization and beyond. I look forward to making a transition to a new, Third Age environment and to developing a portfolio career after I have left.

We are approaching a definition of 'best practice'. In our researches and studies we have come across some very enlightened examples of what might be termed 'best practice' in particular fields. The next three chapters set out relevant suggestions, and Part II describes some interesting examples of the action taken by certain companies which we consider to be models for other companies wishing to excel in all aspects of Third Age transition, from the commercial, motivational and social standpoints. They demonstrate some of the benchmarks against which other companies should compare their own performance.

6

MANAGING CAREER TRANSITIONS

❖

The world of employment has changed radically over the years, so that it is now considered a distinct disadvantage to have worked with only one or two companies during a main career. Consequently the impetus for job change, within a defined career framework, is personal advancement through varied experience; younger people are intent on gaining the necessary enhancements to their c.v. as early and as quickly as possible. The qualities of commitment and loyalty to one organization no longer count for much, because the career timespan has telescoped dramatically. A career start in a person's early 20s is now likely to end, at least on a directly employed basis, in their early 50s, if not before. So the average career span in the employed status has reduced from around 45 years (20 to 65) down to 29 years (23 to 52) in something like only 20 to 25 years. This has necessitated accelerated advancement within companies for those who are ultimately going to take up leading management positions. But what about the average performer?

At present the frequency of job change decreases as the person gets older, and, given appropriate motivational support, there is a reluctance to make any further moves at age 40 plus. In addition, there are still those who have not moved around quite so much and have worked their way through a company from the early days of their career, if not from the start. This presents a company with a dilemma, which, it has to be admitted, few organizations seem to be able to cope with satisfactorily. All the development emphasis is normally concentrated on those under 40, as firms recognize the benefits of the short-term pay back involved. It is much more problematical with people aged 40 plus, because:

o   companies are generally committed to a progressive slimming down, and employees aged 40 plus (50 plus until recently) represent the most obvious target for downsizing

o   there may be some doubt as to the personal ambitions, competence and future job potential for the individuals concerned; they therefore need to fully consider whether or not they should be continuing their career within that organization

○   a potential mismatch between the requirements of the organization and the aspirations of the individual employee may well occur, which is a state of affairs that may fester and needs addressing.

Regrettably there is an almost irreconcilable conflict between the aims and objectives of the corporation, as distinct from the individual, in this. These differences can be summarized in the following:

Company intention	*National or personal need*
in conflict with	
○ Release mature employees to reduce numbers and costs quickly.	○ Increase the national activity/employment rates for older people.
○ Remove mature employees from the payroll at the earliest opportunity.	○ Apply the skills and experience of older people where most beneficial.
○ Avoid recruiting anyone over 45.	○ Create jobs for Third Agers which make sound use of their energy and talents.
○ Concentrate on recruiting, motivating and developing younger employees.	○ Invest in mature employees, who are available, rather than younger people who are in short supply.

We have met people in their 40s who have been very distressed that their company no longer wants them and is not even prepared to keep them on until they can draw a pension at age 50. For the individual concerned it suddenly brings into focus the dramatic question 'What do I want to do with the rest of my life?'. Though there may be a conflict of objectives between the two parties we believe that companies have a responsibility to alleviate, in so far as is practicable, the personal distress that is likely to occur if such a discontinuation of employment becomes a reality. In our view these corrective measures need to be addressed early as part of a career management process.

From the research we have carried out, and from our personal experience with individuals suffering enforced transition, we observe that two main themes are emerging with regard to best practice in the career management area:

○   Individuals should be made aware of their own, personal responsibility for career management at the earliest opportunity, and should take active ownership of issues arising as their career moves forward within the organization. They should not be looking solely to their firm to advance their prospects, but should be taking appropriate steps themselves (with the encouragement and support of the company).

○   Companies should stimulate self-development of the employee through appropriate programmes, linked to a relevant career framework that has been discussed and agreed with the employee at a suitable career review session.

The ideal position, we suggest, is one in which the company and the individual jointly share a mutually beneficial interest in the employee's optimum career development, recognized on both sides. This approach should, of course, include the final transition of moving out of the company into a Third Age career of some kind.

We have noted earlier that this career transition issue has been brought into sharp prominence because of the increasing number of people who find themselves persuaded to leave or retire early in their 40s or early 50s. For example, we know of one senior banking executive who is leaving his bank unwillingly at 54, in the apparent full bloom of his career, at the height of his capability and experience. It has been a complete surprise to him, yet it would not have been if the appropriate career management procedures covering this eventuality had been in place.

There are two distinct components to the effective management of transitions throughout a person's career, therefore. On the one hand, progress will depend to a degree on initiatives taken by the employee, and, on the other, by the level of encouragement and support given by the company to develop or change direction at relevant stages. It bears repeating here that we are talking not only about a transition to a Third Age portfolio, but about the career path that anyone might take after joining a firm, and particularly from the time when they reach the age of 40.

In terms of best practice, we are drawing attention separately to the two phases in a career, relating first to mainstream career development, and second to mature career management (broadly coincident with the periods pre- and post-age 45 or thereabouts). The features of desirable best practice that we would suggest follow in the remainder of this chapter.

MAINSTREAM CAREER DEVELOPMENT

There are a wide variety of programmes operated by companies to suit their own circumstances, and it would be inappropriate for us to go into detail here; the topic could justify another complete volume, as it is a vital component of any company's personal development strategy. Our main task is to describe the requisite features of procedures that will help to achieve the medium- and long-term aims set out in the preceding chapters.

We have come across only one scheme, recently introduced by Guinness, that places sufficient emphasis on the following features:

O   a coherent development programme that covers activities both at work and at home

O   assistance with the development of a personal career plan, embracing agreed aspirations where possible

O   a regular review of achievements against the plan, and the learning that has taken place

O   an emphasis on self-development, which is the foundation of the whole programme.

This imaginative programme is described more fully in Chapter 9.

It would require a great upheaval, though, for a company to introduce such a programme from scratch, as it properly relates to the whole of someone's career; to introduce it piecemeal would be less effective and could perhaps be counter-productive. The advice we would offer to a company in this situation would be to tackle the priority population, probably those aged 40 to 45, by giving them selectively a special career review as a one-off activity. We have called this programme 'Future Directions', because it involves helping people to define, assess and plan ahead their future targets and actions covering the last stages of their main career and, if they wish, their move into the Third Age. The main features of the programme are described below.

WHY SPECIAL CAREER REVIEWS?

There are many reasons why a review may be appropriate at this stage in a person's career. These include uncertainty about future direction, dissatisfaction with current role and prospects, lack of a clear understanding between the individual and company about roles and the impact of potential changes and future options. There is often a clear need to re-establish a sense of purpose and direction at such a critical stage in the person's career, both in their interest and that of their employer.

These often unspoken concerns need to be drawn out by a sensitive and pragmatic process. The approach developed has been seen by companies to complement existing appraisal systems in this context. By using an external facilitator, the programme presents a valuable opportunity for a positive dialogue to take place between the individual and the company. The company may be uncertain about the desired and potential career paths for that person, as may be the individual himself or herself. The programme therefore aims to overcome a reluctance to air issues and concerns by creating a supportive process which involves a mutual agenda for determining a positive future direction, whatever that direction may be.

THE FUTURE DIRECTIONS PROGRAMME

The programme should be spread over a number of weeks to allow a sequence of personal assistance initiatives to take place. The main components of the programme are featured in Figure 6.1.

Introductory session

The introductory session would normally involve the individual's manager (at least initially) and the external facilitator who would lead the subsequent workshop. The purpose of this session is threefold:

○   to explain to the candidate the content and logic behind the career review programme, and to ensure that he or she understands the ultimate purpose and opportunity that it affords

○   to introduce the workshop that will be taking place shortly, and to provide relevant preparation material

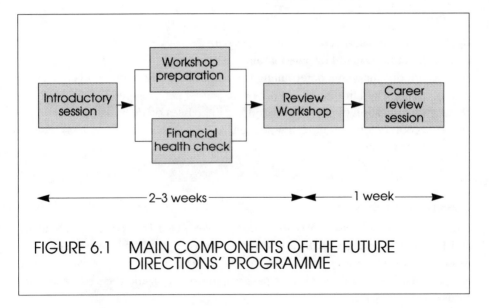

FIGURE 6.1   MAIN COMPONENTS OF THE FUTURE
DIRECTIONS' PROGRAMME

O   to draw the attention of the candidate to the benefits of reviewing his or
       her personal financial situation with the help of a professional financial
       adviser (many companies retain independent specialists to cover this
       aspect), prior to the workshop.

Workshop preparation/financial review

The candidate should prepare himself or herself in the period before the workshop, which should stimulate the thinking process in relation to their current job
situation, and to wider life and career issues. The candidate should therefore begin
the workshop with the following personal data available:

O   a preliminary diagnosis of the job situation and future career priorities
O   views of partner
O   an updated personal profile
O   an assessment of future financial requirements.

Review workshop

The workshop, ideally held in a country hotel, would normally last for one and a
half to two days, depending on the number of participants. The main topics would
include:

Day one

O   introduction, hopes and fears
O   review and development of the preliminary analyses carried out during the
       preparation phase
O   consideration of current and future pressures, needs and opportunities in
       terms of job performance and personal challenges

Day two

O   taking stock, based on all inputs to date
O   identification of key personal aims
O   options mapping; determining the range of realistic routes and choices
O   ranking and firming up on options
O   identification of constraints, and key influences on decision making
O   action before career review session
O   preparation of a document as an advance input to the session.

Career review session

The career review session would normally take place between the candidate and his or her manager (with a relevant specialist if applicable) soon after the workshop, ideally during the following week. The company participants will have had the benefit of the advance personal information, and the session should focus on:

O   the candidate's preferred options for the future
O   determining which of these are realistic
O   discussing the practical implications, such as timing, related to staying in
         the same job or making a career shift
O   confirming development needs in this context
O   agreeing to follow-up action.

The session should be summarized subsequently by the manager, and written confirmation given to the candidate of the agreed outcome.

BENEFITS OF THIS APPROACH

Both the company and the individual should gain considerably from such a pro-gramme, particularly if it is skillfully introduced on the basis of a universally applic-able criterion, e.g. age 45.

The company should gain principally from exploring with the candidate difficult issues in a structured way that might otherwise be embarrassing, or even imposs-ible (without serious damage to morale). The external facilitator can help to make the whole process a positive experience for all concerned, and to stimulate new ideas about future possibilities.

The candidate should benefit from being able to take stock, with the advantage of professional assistance, and to map out a future path that will be acceptable to himself or herself, to his or her partner and to the company. The person concerned should be able to emerge from the process with an enhanced motivation, even if former, unspoken aspirations are shown to be unrealistic.

MATURE CAREER MANAGEMENT (leading to Third Age transition)

If the approach outlined above is adopted, an employee's career beyond age 45 should be set on the right path, and should lead to a relatively smooth transition into a Third Age portfolio at the appropriate time. Unfortunately, that is rarely the case. The task facing most companies is to manage and motivate mature employees in an optimum way, yet be prepared to release them should the economic climate and other commercial considerations provoke such action.

We have found that it is this *preparation* for the Third Age that is sadly lacking in many organizations. All too often we have come across distressed employees who have had no preparation or guidance for the next phase in their lives. A recent example is a professional man aged 48 who has been made redundant by his bank after having worked successfully for the organization for 16 years. Quite suddenly he has been given three months' notice, yet is only 13 months short of qualifying for a pension at 50. Naturally, as a result, he is at his wits' end to know what to do for the best; the speed of the whole experience has been quite alarming for him. Fortunately there are companies that operate in a more positive way, to counter this sad situation, and best practice examples are described in Part II of this book.

However, we believe that the key to a positive and effective transition from a main career into the Third Age lies in the preparation that is carried out beforehand. An employing organization has an excellent opportunity of facilitating this process to mutual advantage. Surprisingly, perhaps, one of the obstacles to genuine preparation is the conventional pre-retirement course offered by a considerable number of companies. We have reviewed many such programmes and have found that a course is generally based on the assumption that the person is retiring (because he or she will be in receipt of a pension) and that the themes of hobbies, health, leisure and money dominate the sessions involved. We consider that the image, language and content is quite wrong, the theme counter-productive to new ideas, and the whole process misleading. It tends to reinforce the view that a person's working days are over, and that the wind down to dependence and decline has already begun.

You will meet many Third Agers on holiday whose main topics of conversation are the remarkable features of past holidays and the eagerness with which they are looking forward to the next; when challenged, they admit that they have not achieved a satisfying Third Age lifestyle. Yet we believe that this represents for the majority an ideal opportunity to start a new life phase; it is a chance 'to live twice'. Consequently conventional pre-retirement courses are now outdated, we suggest, and need to take more account of the development of portfolio careers. Whoever heard of someone leaving a company aged 50 retiring? But the average age of those receiving a pension is already 52, and it is a ludicrous misnomer from the past. We hope that this book will play its part in influencing people away from historical stereotyping and obsolete concepts.

So the essence of mature career management should be optimum motivation in the final stages of a main career, and preparation well in advance for the move to the Third Age. Employees approaching the Third Age need the support of their firm if they are to make a satisfactory transition, as emphasized throughout this book. If left entirely to themselves they are likely to settle for the minimum, and to live unexciting and unfulfilled lives in their Third Age. Most of us need the stimulation of others when dealing with such critical issues, which is why we place so much stress on the need for transition support.

What form should this support take? In our experience, following an introductory session, the heart of the process should be a workshop (either alone, with a partner or a group) that helps the participant(s) to look at themselves, at their innermost wants, and consequently to determine their future priorities. A mistake that many mature people make is to concentrate solely on trying to get another employed job (by drawing up an impressive c.v., answering adverts., etc.) and thereby missing the whole point of Third Age transition. They then tend to become disillusioned rather rapidly, as rejection follows rejection, yet they might have been exploring other routes which could lead to a more satisfying portfolio of activities.

We set out below our view of the supportive framework required to enable such a creative output to be achieved.

INTRODUCTORY SESSION

This session takes place with a facilitator who would subsequently be involved in leading a workshop, and it provides an opportunity for creating a positive image of the potential that exists for the participant in his or her Third Age. The session will aim to:

○ help deal with any feelings of hurt and rejection
○ boost morale by identifying future prospects
○ raise the topic of financial counselling, and ensure that advice is available
○ prepare the participant for a forthcoming workshop, and hand over relevant material
○ encourage the person to attend with their partner (if they have one)
○ reassure the participant of continuing support, as applicable.

The individual or couple should therefore feel fully supported as a result of this process, and be looking forward to the workshop that they will be attending.

TRANSITION WORKSHOP

The workshop can be held for just one person or as many as twenty and the venue and timescale will be modified to suit the circumstances. The number of facilitators will also be adjusted accordingly; the minimum is normally one male and one female counsellor with an appropriate blend of experience. The main themes would normally be:

Loss and change

Participants are introduced to the programme, to each other, and to the positive nature of the Third Age experience for countless people who have preceded them in this experience. They will have the chance to reflect on the social and demographic changes taking place, the impact of these changes on work and on organizations, and the implications for themselves.

Strengths, skills, qualities, satisfactions

The session is mainly about self-knowledge. It is surprising how little most of us know about ourselves, about our deep-seated aspirations, our skills and values, and what really motivates us in practice. By looking back at events and activities that we found fulfilling in the past we can start to discover what is likely to satisfy us in the future. This is not as easy as it sounds, since it involves digging well below the surface and reflecting on the past. To facilitate this process participants complete a life map as part of their preparation for the workshop, indicating significant life events, influences and satisfactions. Enjoyments need remembering in the context of specific occasions or relationship circumstances which were (or are) particularly pleasing in the areas of family life, work, leisure activities, friends, etc. This helps to determine relevant personal characteristics which could be of value during a person's Third Age. Self-examination, often beneficial in itself, generally provides a list of positive features of which the participant was previously unaware. A mix of group activity and individual face-to-face talks produces remarkable results; even the most faint-hearted will normally begin to acknowledge the wide range of talents that they possess.

Aim in life and vision for the future

To what end should these personal strengths and skills be applied? Everyone has a sense of the underlying values and priorities for their lives; even if they are not apparent to the individual they are there, guiding the unconscious. At this transition stage there is the opportunity to state, or to redefine, personal goals for the next life phase, just as one would do with a business. It is important to return to fundamentals, as perhaps one did when considering what to study after leaving school, or whether to study at all. The transition also has similarities with getting married; it is a key step, with important ramifications, and both the bride and groom will have their personal aims and expectations (which are frequently unspoken and dissimilar!).

The advent of the Third Age offers a chance to find out what is in our heart and to identify more closely with ourselves. Such a process may never have been experienced before, but, with skilled assistance, participants have found it invaluable to articulate their current aim in life in this way. The stated aims may include, for example, the following:

O   to maintain an active business life until it is no longer possible physically
O   to become financially independent (defined with personal parameters)
O   to give and receive love, particularly within the family (and therefore spend more time with them!)

o   to establish closer social relationships
o   to give time to new, charitable initiatives in the local community.

It is generally helpful for participants to draw up a statement of their aim in life; two examples taken from Future Perfect courses are as follows:

> My aim in life is to develop an active part-time business role, to spend more time with my family, and to enhance my leisure and recreational interests jointly with my partner.

> My aim in life is to fulfil my gifts and opportunities, working to my strengths and improving my weaknesses, broadly in the service of others and bringing up a caring next generation.

Each 'aim in life' statement should be very personal. It should articulate particular longings and set down realistic markers for the future. As with a business, there is much more chance of achieving your aims if the goals have been clearly identified. One participant in a particular workshop, a banker, described this process as being, for him, a cathartic experience.

vision – wants and aspirations

A group process is used to stimulate the articulation of hidden aspirations, and to develop a whole range of potential activities and pursuits that may, either recently or from some time in the past, be highly sought after by the individuals concerned. Defining an aim in life is all very well, but it can be intangible; it is a broad statement of goals, but doesn't give any indication of the route or activities required to achieve them. Then it is possible to convert this desire to achieve into a manageable list of potential wants.

The list should include all those opportunities which were undeveloped in earlier life, such as playing the cello, learning to ride, building a boat, writing a novel, living in the country, constructing a pottery, etc., as well as the more serious, up-to-date wants connected with business, education or charitable work. The main object of this session is to enable participants to draw up the longest possible list, and to include some surprises that had never been considered before. It is frequently those surprises that provide the key to the future.

Once the list is complete (though there should always be room for additional thoughts) introduce some order by prioritizing the wants, so that the participant is not faced with an impossible task. Considerable care and attention needs to be given to this sifting process; time is required to mull over the practical implications, though it is important that people do not get cold feet by putting imaginary obstacles in their path. The workshop structure is intended to generate maximum self-confidence in the pursuit of their identified wants, and a mutually supportive arrangement encourages participants to avoid imposing false limitations on their aspirations (frequently referred to as 'knocking the monkey off its perch').

What opportunities are there?

At a suitable stage in the programme it is helpful to introduce an inventory of the potential activities that might be possible, so as to jog participants' minds into thinking laterally about the use of the talents that they have come to realize they possess. We have drawn up a simple summary for use as a framework to explore a variety of life and career opportunities in different fields, excluding conventional full-time or part-time employment, as set out below:

O   Act as an Independent Agent
     – use specialist skills and experience
     – set up and operate from 'home office'
     – become self-employed
     – join up with others to form a team?
     – register with appropriate intermediaries, including company associate register if it exists

O   Set up own business in new field
     – antique shop?
     – grass-cutting or gardening?
     – wedding cakes?
     – property refurbishment?
     – craft shop?

O   Use career skills in new ways
     – become a Trainer or Mentor in own specialism
     – join relevant Committees as an adviser
     – become involved with a suitable business activity, possibly as a 'business angel'
     – gain Non-Executive Director appointments

O   Learn new skills or roles
     – train to become a counsellor
     – become a teacher in adult education
     – take a degree or other suitable course
     – join the Open College of the Arts

O   Take up role in the community
     – Justice of the Peace
     – Local Authority, Health Authority appointments
     – support local cause

O   Get involved with a Charity
     – examine local and national opportunities for community work
     – launch a new branch of a national charity, e.g. Home Start or Carr Gomm Society
     – start up local venture, e.g. for the Homeless

O   Develop Hobbies
     – build a workshop or pottery
     – re-layout a garden
     – take up mountain biking
     – turn the hobby into a business?

O   Sport, Travel and Leisure
     – plan new initiatives
     – join a fitness club, walk often

- read more, play a musical instrument
- go to or participate in concerts, theatre, ballet

Choice and commitment

Once all the possibilities have been explored and an agreed list drawn up, the prior-itized wants are turned into practical options which can be developed as real ventures or projects. These may be very diverse, from setting up a new business to improving the relationship with a member of the family, from enrolling for a degree programme to extending and refurbishing a house, from learning to play bridge to setting up a personal computer, printer, fax, etc. in one's home. The breadth of the opportunities that people seize is quite remarkable; frequently they surprise even themselves!

Each main option requires exploring and defining in some detail at this stage, particularly those connected with career or family. The key steps for each option should be set out in an ordered way, and all the prioritized wants (covering differ-ent areas of life) recorded on a single document; this should form the basis of a life plan which will apply over the next two to three years.

We believe it important for partners to develop their choice of options indepen-dently of each other up to this point, and the group work is orchestrated to achieve this end. The purpose of this arrangement is to allow sufficient space for ideas to develop beyond the established pattern of the relationship. Once the framework of choices has been developed, it is possible for a couple to share their ideas and reach some amicable conclusions. For example, one husband was intent on sailing, whilst his wife wished to open up a studio for painting; after discussion they agreed that they should move house straight away to somewhere near a river or sea, with enough accommodation for a studio. The process should enable less forceful participants to reveal their heartfelt wishes, and to be listened to by their partner.

Drawing up and implementing the plan

The final stage involves drawing up detailed plans for the options chosen earlier. These can be developed separately or jointly by any couples involved, depending on the nature of the projects or activities. The main purpose is to set down realis-tic milestone targets for each main project, so that progress can be monitored as the projects are implemented over the coming months. Each activity should be noted within a given time frame just as one would with a conventional business project (even if the aim is to improve a relationship); it is surprising how many executives fail to apply beneficial business disciplines in their personal lives. Once these plans have been completed, the next task is to ensure that they are carried out in practice. Time is normally spent in discussing the best way to achieve this; regular reviews of some kind are a necessary part of the process, and some couples have found that an agreed reward in the form of a night out is a suitable incentive.

OTHER FORMS OF TRANSITION SUPPORT

We have emphasized the personal development process outlined above because we have found it to be the most important element in Third Age transition and it is normally unavailable to the majority of those leaving their main career. There are other aspects that a company might wish to introduce as a supportive aid such as the following:

O   Leaving event, with appropriate recognition for long-term employees. The significance of this rite of passage is frequently undervalued. Our research has indicated the importance for the individual in relation to self-esteem; we know of a recent instance where the manager concerned had to organize and pay for a leaving party because the organization had failed to do so.

O   Pensions and other financial enhancements, which may be developed solely for a particular leaving programme as an inducement to participate. The burning issue at present is the need to arrive at some form of bridging or compensation for those in their 40s who do not yet qualify for a discounted pension at 50. A reduction in the number of discounted years can be used as an instrument to benefit those who have reached the age of 50. We would encourage companies, in conjunction with their financial advisers, to seek new forms of pension arrangement, such as phased annuities through a money purchase scheme, which permit greater flexibility when an employee leaves. We would like to see a situation in which it would be possible to take out a partial pension on leaving, with the balance deferred to a given time in the future.

O   Part-time work through the company's associate register, examples of which are described in subsequent chapters. This we believe to be the single most beneficial arrangement that a company could institute for its employees to support their transitions.

O   Business development advice, where there is a declared intention to set up in business. Various forms of support, including specific training courses, can be made available.

O   Outplacement support, particularly for those employees who wish to find another employed job. However, we believe that this process can lead to unrealistic and unfulfilled expectations arising.

Companies generally pay most attention to the financial package that an employee will be receiving, either directly or indirectly, and this package is certainly important. They perceive that the employee has to leave with his or her self-esteem as intact as possible and money is used to achieve a mutual recognition of this factor. Money alone is inadequate, however, and the psychological benefits that can be achieved (at minimal cost) from a more comprehensive and balanced programme are strongly recommended. Practical examples from a number of prominent organizations are described in Part II.

REWARD MANAGEMENT

Alongside this whole process of career management and development for mature staff, the reward should be examined. Reward should be distinguished from remuneration and compensation, because man 'does not live by bread alone' and as he gets older has different needs, which smart employers will recognize and design reward systems around. One of the authors presented a paper on this topic at the 1990 IPM Conference (*Attracting and motivating the financially secure employee* by John McLean Fox), and identified features valued by mature staff, such as the freedom to 'do their own thing', flexible working arrangements, mix of activities within and without their firm, a balance between work and personal interests, and, of course, a supportive plan for moving into the Third Age.

We believe that mature employees are looking for unusual and imaginative offerings as part of their reward package, which might well be less costly for the employer. Silver power, or the grey revolution, has existed for a long time, but, since reward is a cost to the employer as well as a receipt to the employee, there must be a strong business case for Third Age employment and associated rewards.

For 25 years pay systems rewarded people for doing more important jobs at higher responsibility levels in a formal, more or less hierarchical, organization structure through which they rise, generally speaking, as they get older. With sloppy thinking and practice this can translate into thinking that getting older is what we pay people for, rather than for a contribution to the business. Another fallacy is that cash remuneration is a full and appropriate measure of a person's worth. However, if you ask Third Age employees what they wish to be rewarded for, then it is for many more than to have cash as a crude proxy of their worth as a human being and as a contributor to the workforce.

Company policy and practice, and rigid assumptions about what motivates people or what is appropriate, tend to guide reward in the Third Age at the present time. Gaps between a realistic policy and current practice need to be examined and closed. Clues lie not in broad policy but in creative application in individual cases. It is not necessarily sensible to introduce general reward policies that discriminate in favour of Third Agers, but rather there is a requirement for imaginative and thoughtful application of philosophies, principles and design of contracts to suit individual circumstances.

There is a need to recognize that the Third Age revolution, and the career and managerial revolutions, have been taking place at the same time as several other kinds of revolutionary change; in information technology, services, marketing, communications, careers, etc. One feature we have observed is that personal values, company image and beliefs are very much more important to Third Agers than to the average employee; they have had time to exercise mature judgements in this regard. It is a myth that Third Agers can make much money from multiple retainers or multiple directorships; it is, however, a fantasy common to many executives approaching early retirement.

Vive la différence! Compensatable factors for Third Agers are different from Second Age ones, including: relevant and applicable experience, contacts, interpersonal skills, perceptiveness, wisdom, team collaboration and participation skills, stability in the sense of consistency and persistence, and an understanding and experience of those markets, interests and consumer priorities of the Third Agers themselves. There is undoubtedly a lack of management skill and training among younger managers in the task of leading older workers. Most management and supervisory training still assumes a hierarchical authority and accountability framework. Mature people expect, or deserve, a more enlightened approach. Changes are required, from a hierarchical, paternalistic management style to one that is more of a business partnership, away from the master/servant relationship to one where the contracted supplier of labour or knowledge services is an equal partner with the core firm in getting the work done. This we believe to be the pattern for the future in which the Third Ager can prosper.

It is expedient to consider the total costs of employment, and the significant burden that a full-time employee exerts on the organization. During full-time employment it is acknowledged that the cafeteria principle, with a range of flexible benefits, is appropriate. In managing a transition to the Third Age, however, would it not be possible to extend those considerations more imaginatively, and perhaps to introduce reward aspects that are directly related to the employee leaving at a given point in time? There could, for example, be an optional arrangement for an employee to be given (or buy at a favourable rate) a personal computer, already loaded with suitable programmes and including a training package, so that he or she would be fully prepared to operate a home office when they started their portfolio career. The authors speak feelingly of the deep-felt nature of this requirement. Something like this would not cost a company much money, but would be a practical demonstration that Third Age transition had been considered and relevant action taken on behalf of the employee.

The Ford EDAP programme, referred to in Chapter 14, whereby employees are encouraged to take up extramural programmes and activities, is an excellent example of a practical initiative being introduced, which has both achieved demonstrable results and fostered harmonious employer/employee relationships. (It is a joint initiative with the trade unions at Ford.) We consider that the best employers will actively be seeking to introduce such imaginative approaches in this whole area in future, so as to counter the negative features of Third Age transition and to motivate mature employees by responding to their needs as they prepare themselves for their new life phase.

7

THE SKILLBASE CONCEPT

❖

Thinning out layers of middle management is sometimes a necessary but extremely costly measure in both financial and human terms. IBM(UK) has developed an alternative format that retains former managers and professional staff as independent part-time consultants. It is rapidly becoming a recognized best practice model of Third Age transition at work. Skillbase Ltd was developed and established by IBM in 1990 to market the expertise of men and women who have taken early retirement, generally former managers and professionals in their early to mid-fifties, though the scope of the concept can embrace a wider population.

Older managers could well despair today as they are bombarded by ever more frequent comments and articles suggesting that the 1990s is the decade of management redundancies. With 5 000 management redundancies announced at British Telecom, 1 000 at BP and 4 500 at Philips, not to mention DEC, British Aerospace, Ford and London Underground, it would be easy to assume that middle managers are a species doomed to become extinct. Some blame the recession, and it would be true to say that the recession has exaggerated the trend, but the underlying causes are the need for higher efficiency, cost cutting and new technology.

IBM's manpower planning function forecast that staff numbers would have to be held in the early 1990s, and that it would no longer be possible to recruit additional young graduates. The age profile of employees was therefore in danger of becoming distorted, and ceasing the recruitment of younger staff was unacceptable. The company therefore decided to accelerate their early retirement programme.

A survey of mature employees within IBM revealed that they were not at all eager to retire early, despite adequate financial provision. The main reason was a fear of 'falling over the cliff-edge'. They did not want to suddenly find themselves retired with the biggest decision of the day being what to have for lunch. With regard to prospective activities, their employees fell into two main categories; those deciding to retire but wanting a gradual run-down rather than a 'jump off the cliff', and those wishing to set up as a consultant, establish a new business or work for a charity.

In addition, IBM did not want to lose the skills of their experienced people. They realized that they needed to retain access to the scarce skills of their long-serving and experienced people, but at the same time that it was these same people that they needed to remove from the company. A continual set of retirement offers was producing diminishing returns and IBM needed to increase the take-up rate for any new offer. It was clear that to increase the lump sums offered was no solution. Realizing too that such a reduction was more than an isolated programme, any variation in the lump sum would generate an expectation for the future and help the waverers put off their decision.

Something new was needed, so a collection of ideas from many sources was assembled into what became the Skillbase programme. Skillbase offers a number of days' employment for one or two years following early retirement, and capitalizes on these talents by marketing the capability more widely.

FEATURES

Skillbase is an independent limited company owned 40 per cent by IBM and 60 per cent by its full-time employees. It has been set up as a strictly commercial venture.

Initially, staff aged from 53 in IBM were offered early retirement, and were guaranteed 90 days' work per year for two years by Skillbase. The division or department for which they were currently working were expected to specify the work and request Skillbase to supply suitable people. The costs of the 90 days' work were met from existing budgets covering outside work and temporary staff, thus Skillbase did not add to operating costs when the scheme was initiated.

Under these conditions staff are then able to earn approximately the same amount of money as before; 50 per cent through their pension, 10 per cent through a lump sum yield and 40 per cent through 90 days' work for Skillbase. The net outcome is that staff are able to maintain their level of earnings, yet have to work for only 90 days in the year, with the opportunity of earning more if desired. If the offer levels are lower, as has been the case on several subsequent occasions, then the earnings levels will be proportionately lower.

People joining Skillbase join one of two registers. The 'A' register is where people are normally offered 90 days' work for two years and are paid at a daily rate of $\frac{1}{225}$th of their former salary. They are charged out at this same rate plus National Insurance (NI) and a management fee for the service, which provides Skillbase with its foundation. The 'B' register, which is more flexible, offers no guarantee of work, but the rates are normally higher because the work is related to market demand rather than the offer conditions under the 'A' register. The skills and experience capabilities of each registree are carefully recorded on a database, so that client requirements can be readily accessed via their sophisticated computer system; a short list of potential consultants to meet a request for a given capability in a given industry sector can be drawn up within minutes.

Skillbase is operated by a small team with a team of twelve business managers selling the resource to user clients. They are located in Edinburgh, Manchester, the

Midlands, Vienna, Saudi Arabia and the south of England, and are expanding all the time. The business managers are responsible for all client operations in their particular area.

The Skillbase concept is appealing to other organizations who now offer their early retirers or redundant managers/professionals Skillbase membership; the terms may well be different, e.g. 60 days for one year rather than 90 days for two years, and the age range of the registrees has also varied. In certain circumstances people still in their 30s or 40s have joined, so that a bridge to their next employment situation has been provided by their former employer.

Gradually Skillbase is expanding its range of capabilities and is well placed to develop a range of specific consultancy and training products in the longer term which will compete with traditional providers. The provision of a wide range of experienced and skilled people with an initial work commitment has enabled Skillbase to select and train its own sales force and to enter the general management consultancy market.

Almost immediately from its start up, skills were recruited from outside IBM and today Skillbase can offer a range of more than 4 000 experienced people who can tackle almost any aspect of a company's operation; only a quarter of these are former IBM employees. This consultancy works alongside IBM in the market-place and is proving to be a very successful operation, capable of delivering skills across the widest areas and geographies at modest prices.

In addition Skillbase now runs IBM's training centre at New Place in Hampshire. It is responsible for providing IBM with relevant programmes under contract, and has been able to achieve this at a cost of a third less than before by making optimum use of part-time specialists on their registers as trainers. These training programmes are now marketed widely in the UK, with the benefit of IBM's pedigree attached to them.

Skillbase has exceeded expectations. After the first year of operating, revenue had exceeded £5 million with a sensible profit level being achieved on this figure. Subsequently turnover has virtually doubled in the second and third years, and the number of registrees is growing fast as more companies (one of the more notable being British Telecom) take advantage of this facility. Skillbase has handled contracts in IT and banking in the Gulf and for training in Portugal and Turkey. It has worked in 19 countries so far – from Trinidad to Mongolia. Skillbase consultants have been involved in reorganizing office space for a high street retail chain, evaluating pay for a newly privatized industry, and have regular work with NHS Trust hospitals. The rate of growth in terms of business gained and members taken on is continuing apace and the whole experience has proved extremely positive for IBM, for the client companies involved, and the individuals directly concerned.

BENEFITS

The retirees find this kind of approach very welcome indeed. It fulfils their needs for immediate part-time involvement and removes many of the fears about suddenly leaving a workplace where they have been secure for so long. At the same time it has provided reassurance for the one or two years after the change that work will be available for a given number of days per year, with the potential of further work still. Skillbase has enabled people to move smoothly through the transition period into their chosen new roles.

IBM and other companies have also benefited greatly as clients of Skillbase, and it is these corporate, commercial benefits which have been the spur to its rapid growth. Companies only have to pay at the level of salary costs for their Skillbase members since they leave the payroll when retiring. The normal 37 per cent payroll on-cost for benefits is therefore saved, and any savings on accommodation are additional to this sum.

Initial research indicates that staff are most effective when they are able to work on one specific task at a time. With the Skillbase concept each person is allocated just such a specific task and is consequently very much more productive. They are no longer distracted by management or other company activities and can concentrate on the project in hand. The client company therefore benefits from the equivalent of much more than the 60 or 90 days nominally involved.

One of the most beneficial results has been that it becomes possible to reduce core staffing. Ready access to the pool of talent within Skillbase operates in practice as a reserve labour force. It is therefore possible to staff nearer the trough level rather than for peaks, which can represent a very substantial financial saving.

The implementation of this policy of 'phased retirement' has had a very positive effect all round. The younger staff have been pleased to observe the imaginative approach that has been adopted, managers have been delighted with the cost effectiveness of the facility and the early retirers have enjoyed the freedom they now have, linked to a continuing interaction with their former colleagues. We believe that this form of flexible resourcing will be an important feature for the future for all companies.

As John Nicoll, Managing Director of Skillbase, says:

> New problems need new solutions. This is just one example of the development of a new tool to help with a problem that is now likely to become generic. Companies must now consider all the options and a whole range of new ideas if they are successfully to manage this area. This is not a short-term problem and such imaginative approaches will become ever more necessary as the future demonstrates that the manager has an ever shortening life in the large company of tomorrow whilst already scarce skills become scarcer.

In summary, if an organization has older employees who are poorly motivated, performing unsatisfactorily and restricting development, they are likely to be less commercially effective than those who have dealt with the problem imaginatively and implemented the necessary changes. Many companies have started to realize that their mature employees represent a significant investment from which they could obtain a much better return.

8

THE WAY AHEAD

❖

A PRIORITY FOR THE FUTURE

We believe that most companies are mistaken in their attitudes to Third Age issues, and, in particular, to the commercial implications concerning the future prosperity of their organization and its employees. In our five years of specialization in this field we have become very aware of the short-termism which tends to apply when Third Age transition comes up for debate (normally when the next tranche of employees has to be released to achieve immediate downsizing targets). The reaction to such a requirement is often to implement a programme of compulsory or voluntary redundancy in the least painful way (to the company), or, in the better companies, to 'do the decent thing' and provide a modicum of support to those who are leaving.

The message of this book is that *the Third Age revolution is more significant than the average company executive might imagine*, and that the implications for the future should be considered as an important part of corporate strategy. It should be noted that the Carnegie Foundation, with its impeccable reputation in the social responsibility field, has drawn attention to Third Age employment issues (among several others) as being of paramount importance to companies and to the economy as a whole; they have recognized the implications well in advance of most industrial and commercial institutions. It is now the turn of individual companies and other employing organizations, we suggest, to heed the information and experience we have contributed, to their own medium- to long-term advantage.

Third Age transition represents a strategic business challenge which companies have to confront head on in order to remain competitive, through operating a variable cost base that is responsive to market conditions. The fixed, or, more accurately, rising committed long-term costs of Second Age personnel philosophies are inappropriate and unsustainable for the labour and product markets of the late 1990s.

A NEW CULTURE NEEDED

MATURE PEOPLE AND WORK

An Institute of Personnel Management report on 'Policies, Attitudes and Practice towards Age and Employment', concluded that:

> it is clear that an early exit culture has developed across Europe among both employers and employees. This is deeply entrenched and will be difficult to overcome ... one aspect ... is the cost to the countries concerned ... a direct cost to the social security system.
>
> (IPM, 1993)

Part One of the IPM study was undertaken by the University of Sheffield Department of Sociological Studies and looked at comparative data on the employment of older workers in five European countries – Germany, France, the Netherlands, Sweden and the UK in order to identify areas where the sharing of experience could be beneficial. For example both France and Germany, concerned about social and economic costs, have strengthened their legislation to discourage early retirement and age discrimination, without much effect – a sign that the inertia of the early exit culture is considerable and will prove difficult to change.

The conclusions to the study included the following:

> The recession has masked many of the implications of the forecast demographic changes but *eventually organisations will have to come to terms with the need to encourage the continuing economic activity of older workers, many of whom have become accustomed to the view that employees should be able to leave paid employment well before state pension age. Reversing this will require significant changes in practice and a major effort to manage the change in expectation needed in an older workforce to encourage older employees to stay on and be productive.* The cost of the occupational pension provision may help to force the change, although awareness of these costs among employers has been slow to develop.
>
> (ibid.)

Finally, the IPM report suggests that

> it makes good business sense to recruit from the widest labour pool available in order to ensure the widest possible choice of those who can potentially contribute. This also follows for utilisation within the workforce, promotion opportunities etc. If employers, for whatever reason, exclude older workers then, as the research indicates, they face the danger of underutilising what has been shown to be a quantitatively important resource. In addition, as the workforce actually does age, employers lose the continuity and skills which will be vital to success.
>
> (ibid.)

SELF-EMPLOYMENT AND THIRD AGE TRANSITION

One of the interesting and possibly significant findings in policy terms of a number of these recent studies is that older people are considerably more likely to be self-employed than employed people as a whole. At the very least this lends hope to the possibility that the Third Age portfolio career can and does work for those in the second half of life. At best it can point the way to a Third Age economy or a Third Age economic recovery from recession. It is worth noting the success of those companies who have included a genuine and sincere enterprise programme, creating or facilitating self-employed work and small business development programmes for their former employees, such as British Steel, British Coal and IBM to name just three giants.

Throughout the economy there is a more subtle but equally important shift whereby either before or after the event companies are now realizing that, even though they cannot afford and do not need them all of the time, they do have a material continuing need to use the skills of former employees on a subcontract or consulting basis. Those companies, such as IBM and British Telecom with the foresight to anticipate the requirement before the event and to make it a feature of the transition package, have received positive publicity externally and some more sceptical reception internally, particularly from those managers who remain or who would have liked the opportunity and were not offered it. It is not surprising that such a radical transformation in thinking would take some settling down. However, there is evidence that other companies who pursued radical downsizing programmes, such as some of the retail banks, are now quietly having to re-employ on a consultancy basis some of the skills and people that they rather indiscriminately let go.

THE MYTH OF THIRD AGE DETERIORATION

Of course, by definition the fact that somebody is self-employed eliminates at least any internal discrimination on age grounds beyond the more or less healthy self-doubt that seems to drive all successful entrepreneurs. Within companies, research has shown that it is a myth that the older worker is not adaptable or trainable. Successive studies from Professor Peter Warr's Unit at Sheffield, and from other departments of occupational psychology, have shown that differences in capability are as wide within age groups as they are between age groups.

Part Two of the IPM study was undertaken by the Policy Studies Institute, and looked at 19 UK case studies which showed that case study employers tended to see older workers as more reliable, more conscientious, more stable and as having a stronger work ethic. However they also saw them as being more resistant to change, more difficult to train, less healthy and less cooperative: 'The prejudice appears so ingrained as to persist in the face of contradictory experience. This indicates the extent of the education and training process which will be needed if attitudes are to change' (ibid.) These views were held despite evidence in those actual companies to the contrary!

A common prejudice is that older workers' performance and attendance decline and this is frequently used as an excuse for not training or promoting them. The fact is that while certain mental and physical characteristics do decline with age, most organizations do not require people to operate at the limits of their capacities – if only an organization was that good and finely tuned! So it is most unlikely that any minor deterioration in capacities will affect job performance; it is more likely to be enhanced by compensating increases in steadiness and reliability.

The US Department of Labour reported the half life of skills (i.e. point at which 50 per cent of skills have become obsolete) now to be three to five years, thus destroying the argument that it is not cost effective to retain older workers.

MANAGERS NEED EDUCATING

What is needed is 'an educative role to ensure that the facts about older workers' capabilities and ways of optimizing these are given the widest possible publicity'. Some leading companies have used data from their personnel information system to show managers the facts of current Third Age workforce performance and contribution as a way of encouraging them to reconsider their ideas.

At a Future Perfect seminar following publication of the Carnegie Inquiry Reports one eminent personnel director even went so far as to explain in disbelief that it would be quite impossible to do anything about the Third Age problem through personnel management means, even if he wanted to (which he did not), because the company was getting rid of expensive Third Agers and had a duty to favour young people in the employment stakes, if anybody. This view was clearly based on Second Age thinking rather than Third Age awareness!

Part Three of the IPM study was undertaken by Professor Peter Warr of the MRC/ESRC Department of Social and Applied Psychology at the University of Sheffield and looked at the attitudes of personnel managers. Up to 80 per cent believe age discrimination to be a problem and they also exhibited it to some extent themselves. The current prejudicial or pragmatic approach may be against employers' long-term best interests especially if

> in the next century labour surplus gives way to labour shortage ... events in the early 1990s have shown that labour shortages can hit employers in particular regions or sectors even when there is an overall labour surplus ... simply instituting a more open approach to HR management, even if it does not specifically target older workers, can have a beneficial effect.
>
> (IPM, 1993)

Organizations can benefit from changing the way they think about filling jobs and taking a much more proactive approach towards the way they meet their performance targets. The UK is at the forefront of discussions on the implications of future age group variables in the working population, having more examples in the international comparative studies of employers who had recently undertaken initiatives. However, we can learn from Renault in France, who have sought to create a learning environment.

Employers should see the importance of creating a learning environment so that employees are much less likely to enter the later stages of working life unprepared as a result of continuous access to training opportunities that the learning organization brings. Other approaches entail a more strategic approach to human resourcing:

O   rethinking workplace reduction
O   assigning redundant employees to a labour pool to fill vacancies or to complete tasks from which there is usually inadequate labour

O   varying working time rather than releasing people and then having to
         recruit when an upturn comes.

As a result of the delayering that has been taking place there are fewer middle
managers, and a higher proportion of younger managers who are more prejudiced
with more negative views towards older workers. Special retraining and reorienta-
tion is needed to remind these younger managers of the power and the potential
of the experienced employee.

THE EMERGING HR IMPERATIVES

The Towers Perrin Study on 'Priorities for Competitive Advantage', undertaken in
1990 for IBM and based on extensive international research, suggested that the key
business goals for companies in the future would consist of the following:

O   high levels of productivity, quality and customer satisfaction
O   a direct linkage of HR policies with business strategy
O   attraction and retention of quality candidates
O   workforce flexibility
O   strong organizational culture, well articulated and defined
O   employee satisfaction.

The implications of these findings are that HR initiatives will increasingly need to
be responsive to market conditions and global business structures, linked closely to
strategic business plans, and conceived and implemented jointly by line and HR
managers. This will require the personnel function to adopt a more thoughtful,
proactive stance. This implies a shift from industrial relations officers to strategic
business managers, from salary administrators to compensation planners, from
selection interviewers to recruitment marketers, discipline and grievance handlers
to coaches and counsellors, manpower controllers to people developers, trainers
to developers, social egalitarians to market economists, cost reducers to value
adders, establishment men and women to organizational consultants.

There are fixed assumptions within human resource management at the present
time. This research is indicating that there is a desperate need for a more flexible
approach, and a willingness to match human talent with the work to be done in a
much more creative way. As part of this potentially more flexible approach, the
experienced or older manager is not a cause but a component of the human
resourcing map of Europe. Companies which fail to redraw their own Third Age
demography will not survive.

The world map is continually being redrawn by international competitors, and in
order to match them we have to recruit, retain and reward the experienced
employees as part of our competitive advantage and response. The irony is that it
is the reciprocal of Japan. To remain competitive the Japanese can no longer afford
to maintain their much heralded lifelong employment principles. We, on the other
hand, who, in better times, have aspired to create such an environment have
perhaps moved too quickly in the reverse direction and cannot afford to let too
many people go. New ways must be found, new pathways developed through

the Third Age transition for individuals and companies who are the ultimate economic beneficiaries of getting it right, and who bear the financial burden if we
do not.

THE PRIORITIES FOR COMPANIES

In summary we would like to draw attention to the following characteristics which
we believe companies should alert themselves to in considering Third Age issues,
with the objective of being amongst the leading performers in the 1990s and the
early part of the next century:

○   **A mammoth change in career life is already under way**, and
companies should recognize that there will be no return to the conventional
employment patterns of the 1960s, 1970s or even 1980s – it is too expensive
to retain individuals for such a long career span, with all the related costs
that this practice entails. Consequently there will be a much more competitive market for core staff, and a greater reliance on short-term, contract staff.
We are therefore talking about a radical change in a company's future
resourcing strategy, which merits attention at the very highest level.

○   **This resourcing strategy is likely to involve the use of a
committed, flexible cadre of skilled staff**, and we believe that the
operational and commercial benefits that can be obtained from implementing the Skillbase concept are not appreciated by companies. Who
better to work on a project basis than a former employee, if chosen and
managed appropriately? In a particular organization, with a managerial and
professional population of 2 000 (out of a total of 24 000), it would be
possible to release 200 of them, rather than the 100 originally planned, by
applying the Skillbase principles. By these means, with the 200 working in
the company on a part-time basis, it should be possible to save £2.7m in
the first year (instead of £1.7m), and £6.5m in the second year (instead of
£3.5m). There are additional benefits beyond this, but we believe that such
a very attractive commercial outcome, even just in the short term, should
command management's attention as a priority opportunity.

○   **The Third Age policy is an issue for the Chief Executive and
his/her top management team to address**, and should not be confined
to the personnel function. Once the implications can be appreciated at the
highest level it should be possible to generate the appropriate degree of
awareness throughout the managerial and professional ranks, and, in due
course, to develop a Third Age policy such as has been outlined in this book.

○   **Managers and professional staff in their 40s are becoming
disillusioned**, having observed the practice of regular downsizing in
their organization in recent years, with the average age edging down
towards the upper 40s. They are questioning what their current company
has in store for them, once they have passed the age of 40. Why should
they commit themselves to the normal overload and unfavourable

working practices to which they, and the company, have become accustomed? Conventional solutions to this problem are unlikely to succeed, because they have 'heard it all before'. They have seen colleagues apply themselves to the limit, only to be released at relatively short notice as the economic situation changes.

Some more aware companies have already taken some steps in a positive direction, as in the examples described in Chapters 9 and 16. Even then, we suggest, the emphasis has tended to be on improving responses to conventional management action, such as downsizing, which in our view represents Second Age thinking rather than a Third Age vision of the future. We are therefore urging our readers to see the bigger picture if they want to incorporate the full Third Age message, and improve the bottom line for their companies. If a company can take advantage of the approaches we have outlined, to deal with in turn each of the main issues identified, then the company should enhance its long-term profitability (and gladden the hearts of the authors by having made their task worthwhile).

PART II

THIRD AGE TRANSITION IN ACTION: CASE STUDIES

❖

In choosing examples of best practice we have drawn both from our own experience and from recommendations by others in the field. No one organization follows a comprehensive pattern which we could endorse in total as representing best practice, however. What we have tried to do is to identify particular features which have struck us as possessing interesting and imaginative traits which other companies may wish to adapt to their own circumstances. A description of such features is therefore set out for each best practice company concerned.

9

GUINNESS

❖

Guinness has changed from a brewing group based in the UK, Ireland, Nigeria and Malaysia only ten years ago, with low profitability, to an international beverage business with a wide range of brands, from Johnny Walker and Gordons through to Guinness stout. It claims to be 'the most profitable alcoholic drinks company in the world'. The company employs some 24 000 people worldwide.

Its recent corporate history is well known. The controversial takeover of United Distillers was the most significant step in its ambitious diversification and expansion plans. Consequently both Guinness Brewing and United Distillers, the two groupings through which it operates internationally, have experienced very considerable structural and management changes. This process appeared to us, in our 1991 study, to have benefited the attitude to mature employees.

One manager declared 'You won't find any duff older managers around the place', implying that being older was not considered a disadvantage but that the main criterion for retention or advancement was *competence*. A typical comment on this subject was as follows:

> There is nothing in our performance reviews about age, and there is a need for
> mature representation overseas. History and heritage is an important part of brand
> marketing; we have to cultivate the 'not new' image.

In reviewing the organization for this book we were told that the above views were still supported strongly. In addition, some candidates in their 50s had been appointed recently to posts at the centre. It was felt that a number of people would gradually move to a portfolio career, following the example of their Group Personnel Director, Colin George, who now includes chairmanship of the Open College within a new range of activities under development. He saw a pattern of early retirement and moves to flexible careers becoming the norm at Guinness before too long.

The most notable initiative at Guinness, however, concerns the way that self-development has been introduced as a platform for their personal and career development programmes. In the late 1980s Guinness was laying down the framework for more systematic management and career development. This included instigating performance management systems, training managers and subordinates in appraisal, developing core competency training modules and installing a corporate management review system. This approach was effective, but the company felt that it wasn't enough, that they weren't breaking away sufficiently from the posture that management development and career development was something that the company, rather than the individual, should be undertaking.

The company was influenced by the thinking of, among others, Rosabeth Moss Kanter, Professor of Business Administration at Harvard University, who is renowned for her work on innovation and corporate transformation; her books include *The Change Masters, The Challenge of Organisational Change* and *When Giants learn to Dance*. Her view is that 'if organisations need to be focused, fast, friendly and flexible, then we would have to give far more attention to empowering individuals to take responsibility and make decisions – and that means taking responsibility about their own careers as well as other aspects of the business'. Guinness therefore set about achieving the following self-development mind-set within their people:

O   I own my own learning.
O   I am the best project manager for my career.
O   If I don't know, I'll ask.
O   My boss is paid to coach me and help me develop.
O   Other people are there to help me (and vice versa).
O   They can't help me if they don't know what I want.
O   My work is my prime source of learning.
O   Flat and changing hierarchies equals growth and development through the job.
O   As one individually grows and develops, so does the business grow and develop (we are the business).
O   I make my own plans.

This mind-set represented a fundamental shift in attitude for Guinness. They believe that self-managed development involves each person gaining a realistic understanding of his/her own make-up, using that understanding to develop a plan for working towards some personal goals, and harnessing the available resources to help learn and develop appropriately. This programme utilizes a career/self managed development log book entitled *The Right Direction*, which has the subsidiary caption: 'To help individuals think about themselves, their future and how they can realize their potential'.

Each person participating in the programme is given the log book which helps them to monitor progress and includes:
Profile:

O   summary of strengths and weaknesses
O   what really matters to you
O   aspirations
O   record of past learning.

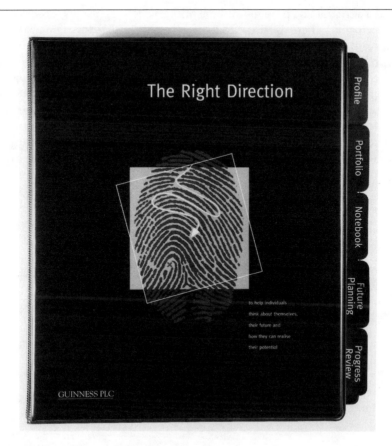

FIGURE 9.1   THE GUINNESS LOG BOOK

Portfolio:

O   experiences/achievements
O   where any output is kept.

Notebook:

O   significant learning events.

Future planning:

O   objectives
O   achieving the objectives
O   potential obstacles
O   action plan.

Progress review:

O   achievements, learning, etc. related to the period under review.

There is a core training programme at Ashridge which represents the starting point for participants. There is also separate assistance given for training people as coaches and developers, which is an important part of the process.

The relevance of this approach to managing career transitions into the Third Age is very considerable. If someone is sufficiently imbued with the self-development philosophy along the above lines, he or she will be formulating aspirations for their Third Age early on. The Third Age, after all, should represent the next stage of career development following a main career, and should be planned for in exactly the same way as a main career phase. In addition, experienced coaching should ensure that this topic is addressed within the future planning and progress review framework. We heartily endorse this approach by Guinness as representing best practice in this field; Guinness is evidently good for you, as the saying goes.

10

KLEINWORT BENSON

❖

The Kleinwort Benson Group is one of the leading merchant banks in the City of London. It currently employs approximately 1 900 people in the UK and 700 overseas. A notable feature of Kleinwort Benson's operation is that it was one of the first organizations to have introduced an Employee Assistance Programme, which it launched in January 1990. This was a remarkably courageous step for a traditional City firm to have taken at the time, and other institutions regarded this move with a considerable degree of interest and, it must be said, some scepticism.

It is worthwhile exploring the reasons for the bank's initiative. The Group has undergone a very significant amount of change since 1985. The long-established stockbroking firm of Grieveson, Grant and Co. joined the Group in 1986 in preparation for Big Bang, which more than doubled the number of staff involved at that time. Since 1988, however, staffing numbers have been reduced by about one third, in common with the general downsizing that has occurred elsewhere in the City; Black Monday was a shock to most institutions and caused a realignment of their businesses. The change, though, for Kleinwort Benson has been becoming an integrated merchant and investment bank, and the upgrading of skills that this has required in order to compete internationally. The bank has to develop particular skills to deal with that more controlled state of affairs. Consequently it has recruited and developed a large number of younger people, the average age dropping in 1988 to 31, with the average length of service of around four years.

Such radical change, with associated restructuring, has meant that all employees have been working in a much more demanding environment. The Group's personnel department had to concentrate on the mechanisms of recruitment, changes in structure, new payment and benefit systems, etc. and felt that they did not know the bank's people as well as before (which is hardly surprising, given the shorter service and the changed population). In these circumstances it was considered that an external counselling service, independently accessible by each employee, would be a very valuable facility.

And so it has proved; the bank has been delighted with the initiative, supplied by Personal Performance Consultants UK Ltd., and believe that it is genuinely tackling the stresses and strains which lie below 'the tip of the visible iceberg'. Kleinwort Benson has found that, though the scheme operates usually on a self-referral basis, it is sometimes able to point the employee in the right direction to ensure that he or she gets the help that may be needed. In certain circumstances the counsellor has approached the bank on the employee's behalf, with their consent, to help resolve a particular issue. The bank therefore sees the three parties working together to provide the maximum benefit for staff.

One specific group of employees that are the beneficiaries of this approach are mature employees aged 45 plus, who may be very concerned about changes affecting them personally, particularly regarding Third Age transition. We therefore believe that access to counselling in some form represents best practice in this area, and it would appear that Kleinwort Benson has led the way in this respect.

In other relevant areas Kleinwort Benson is less ageist than a number of its competitors. The Group has recruited a number of directors in their late 40s, and it recently appointed a director in his 50s to take on a senior European role. Its average retirement age is 57 or 58, which is higher than usual in the City. In career development terms, self-development is becoming an important feature, and staff are involved in a variety of initiatives using distance learning for certain subjects and a management module approach for management development. Transition support for Third Age entry is provided by the bank. It sends people on Future Perfect workshops and has started to experiment with a Skillbase-type arrangement for certain retirees, and encourages groups of such employees to form their own small businesses if it is mutually beneficial.

Of interest is a switch in their pension arrangements in April 1992 from a conventional final-salary-based scheme to a defined contribution plan. Kleinwort Benson believes this to be much more flexible and permits, in particular, Third Agers to arrange the benefits to suit their own circumstances. The bank has also joined the Wellness Forum recently, and is intent on monitoring health as a positive feature in order to enable its employees to achieve more enjoyable and fulfilled lives.

11

SHELL

❖

S hell is recognized as an organization which has an imaginative policy with regard to career development right through into the Third Age. It also has a strong commitment to community initiatives, and one of these, Age Resource, is concerned with promoting fulfilled Third Age living.

Shell UK used to employ some 20 000 people 15 years ago, but now employs only about 10 000. This downsizing, common to most large corporations, has been achieved as a result of new work methods, technology advances and changed structures; the consequent business performance has been very positive throughout this period. Staff have benefited from a very generous severance scheme, and this reduction in numbers has been realized with very little enforced action on Shell's part. The company has tried hard not to allow all the wisdom and experience of mature employees to disappear as a result of this attractive arrangement, and has maintained an appropriate balance through a thorough monitoring of severance requests. Though this scheme has mainly involved people over 50, severances have also affected younger employees. The company strongly supports the concept of their employees starting a second vocational career and the transition to a productive Third Age is therefore viewed as the norm. We regard the fact that this philosophy has become embedded into the culture as being highly significant; it permeates all relevant processes.

There are five main activities which we would draw to your attention as examples of best practice in this field.

CAREER MANAGEMENT AND DEVELOPMENT

Shell has an annual appraisal and reporting system for employees that covers short-term performance aspects, medium-term career prospects and long-term career potential. This is quite unusual; most such procedures concentrate on immediate targets and developments during the next 12 months. Shell, however, makes a significant point of considering the long term on a regular basis, and this topic accounts for a notable amount of space on the appraisal form. Initially the long-term potential appears very indistinct, but as the employee gets older it naturally sharpens up; transition to the Third Age therefore becomes a feature of the discussion as a matter of course, well in advance of the actual event. The style of the appraisal session is to establish a sound relationship between mature adults and exchange views on this basis. Consequently it is normally possible to ensure that realistic outcomes are achieved on both sides. In this way they have been able to minimize any surprises, and transitions to the Third Age can be planned with a high measure of understanding by both employer and employee.

We believe that this approach, if carried out sensitively, represents the optimum in motivational and human terms. It is in direct contrast to the many instances we come across, which, at the extreme, involve early retirement or redundancy starting immediately from the day of notification. Although this has also happened occasionally in Shell, the company has tried where possible to adopt a caring and pragmatic approach.

PREPARATION FOR THIRD AGE TRANSITION

Shell International and Shell UK, which acts as the umbrella organization for exploration, refining and marketing activities in the UK, operate independently and do not necessarily share common policies. In the UK, however, there has been a similar approach to preparation for retirement for quite some time, though this is being modified to allow also for assisting redundant staff below retirement age. It is interesting to note that the average age of retirement in Shell has been the mid- to late 50s in recent years, and is now considered to be in the very early 50s (defined as being those leaving who are in receipt of a pension).

The original platform for retirement preparation has in the main been a two-part programme, the first part occurring at age 50 (ten years before the 'normal' retirement age of 60) and the second during the actual year of leaving. A brief summary of the coverage given is as follows:

O   *Retirement financial planning (2 days)*
     The topics are largely concerned with financial planning (Shell Pension Fund and AVCs, investment, tax and will strategy, insurance/mortgages) but can also include preliminary consideration of future career activities and leisure pursuits. The programme has recently been modified to form a universal 2-day financial planning course which can also be available to staff of all ages who are in a redundancy situation.

O   *Pre-retirement (5 days)*
     The allocation of time between the relevant topics is broadly:
financial issues/planning	2 days
employment and activity	1 day
Shell/retirement issues	1½ days
health	½ day.

There is considerable emphasis on 'taking stock' during this course, i.e. carrying out a life review and determining future priorities.

This programme is being modified to take account of the fact that certain participants will have attended the financial planning course only very recently or are receiving outplacement support, in which case it can be reduced to around three days as part of a total package.

Parts of Shell UK are therefore adapting their approach to suit the prevailing circumstances, and now provide a modular package of support to suit individual needs. In response to certain downsizing activities Shell has set up internal outplacement centres in their main locations, which carry out individual diagnoses as a precursor to implementing a tailor-made programme of support for each person. A very much more flexible system is therefore in operation, though for those aged 50 and over the content is unlikely to vary significantly from that involved in the original programme. It is highly commendable that such a retirement preparation approach has been a regular feature for so many years.

We have also noted that a considerable number of Shell retirers have become involved in the company's community programmes on a part-time basis, particularly Shell Better Britain and Livewire, as part of this process. This is an entirely appropriate use of Shell Third Agers which we very much applaud.

PENSION LIAISON REPRESENTATIVES

Another important role for 40 of Shell Third Agers is a Pension Liaison Representative (PLR). These 40 PLRs cover the whole of the UK, and are paid a salary and expenses for working on a part-time, 3 to 3½ days per week, basis to service Shell's 30 000 or so UK pensioners.

The prime purpose is to act as a contact point for pensioners, to provide them with appropriate information and to visit each person once every 18 months to 2 years. The PLRs are particularly concerned with instances of sickness, frailty and bereavement. The company may well ask a PLR to investigate a specific occurrence so that he or she can advise them on the relevant supportive action that needs to be taken. This Shell 'Aftercare' scheme is valued highly, and is a rare and admirable example of dedicated company support for pensioners who have long since left their main career.

AGE RESOURCE

Shell has an ambitious community relations programme. Probably the two most notable schemes are Livewire, which helps young people to start their own business, and Shell Better Britain, which is committed to improving the local environment. Both these schemes receive thousands of enquiries annually.

Shell UK joined with the Esmee Fairbairn Charitable Trust and Age Concern to launch a project called Age Resource in 1990. The aim of Age Resource is to promote 'active elders' in our society, and to provide a coordinating role for a number of appropriate initiatives. The most prominent of these is an awards scheme, sponsored by Shell, for successful projects in nine categories:

- voluntary work in education
- voluntary work in caring
- voluntary work to enhance the environment
- personal development
- self-help in the community
- inter-generational
- campaigning
- employment
- goodwill.

Age Resource, whose President is the Prince of Wales, is therefore promoting the virtues of Third Age living and demonstrating that growing older can be a time of fulfilment.

SHELL PENSIONERS' ASSOCIATION

The Shell Pensioners' Association (SPA) is now 25 years old. Formed with only 750 members, it currently has over 13 000 (approximately half the 25 000 pensioners eligible) with 20 branches covering most of the UK. It welcomes new members to its ranks; between 70 and 80 per cent of all staff now retiring join the SPA, and deferred pensioners are encouraged to join as they become eligible. There is an equivalent association, the 44 Club, with 6 000 members, for those who are pensioners of the sister company Shell Mex and BP. The SPA aims to keep alive the Shell family spirit and interest in Shell Group activities after retirement. Contact with members is maintained through the quarterly *SPA News*, a publication which covers forthcoming events, branch activities, discussions on pension matters, members' views, and matters of general interest regarding the Group.

The three main areas of activity are as follows:

- *Personal contact*
  Members meet at central and branch activities, which are the hub of the SPA's life. Branches organize a wide array of local events – lunches, theatre visits, film shows and outings. One enterprising branch, for example, organized no less than 24 special outings, holidays or educational events in one year. Branches are self-supporting, and any administration costs incurred are recovered within the branch (though the company may assist through loaning computer equipment to help with this aspect).
- *Pensions*
  Pensions have, in recent years, assumed a much higher profile in the concerns of members than previously. With a significant and increasing proportion of Shell pensioners as members, the SPA, on behalf of its members, maintains an active channel of communication with the Trustee

Board and the Shell companies on pension matters. An important adjunct to the SPA is the Shell Pensioners Benevolent Association (SPBA), a registered charity, which can provide grants or loans for a variety of needs, particularly where there is evidence of poor health and straitened financial circumstances (usually in conjunction with the PLRs referred to above). Such grants have covered hip operations, property problems etc., and members have even left their houses to the SPBA as a contribution to its funds, currently standing at £500 000.

O   *Retirement opportunities*

Shell is very keen that its pensioners should have the maximum opportunity to assist with the initiatives taken by the company in the community. The SPA provides the appropriate vehicle to maintain contact for such projects, and there are instances of a satisfactory involvement in connection with initiatives in the fields of enterprise, education and the environment.

We find these arrangements impressive; this could surely be a reliable model for other companies aspiring to offer appropriate aftercare for their long-serving employees. Shell supports the pensioner activities directly by providing an office in Shell Centre, and pays for four part-time officials, two working three days a week and two working one day a week. The company also enables the quality *SPA News* to be printed and distributed to 13 000 members of the association, which is no small undertaking. It is hardly surprising that members are enthusiastic about this facility.

12
BT

In 1982 British Telecommunications (as it then was) employed some 250 000 people and was one of the largest employers in the UK. One of the main tasks facing the Board in the wake of privatization was the need to reduce this figure through restructuring, which would take full advantage of rapidly changing telecommunications technology and new profit-oriented business units. The way in which these reductions have been progressively achieved in practice is of great interest, since it provides a unique example of an innovative and comprehensive approach to downsizing in this decade.

The workforce stood at 230 000 in 1991; this figure was reduced to 199 000 a year later, 165 000 in 1993 and further, less radical reductions are planned for future years as technology progresses still further. At the start of the release programme (as BT terms it) in 1991, every one of the 230 000 employees was interviewed by their director or manager to explore whether they might be interested in leaving BT under a new voluntary scheme, and, if so, to what extent this might be feasible. This intensive interview programme was carried out over a period of four weeks, which was a considerable feat. The outputs from the interviews provided management with the necessary information to start developing and implementing their first major programme called 'Release 92'; this was followed one year later by 'Release 93', and has developed into a highly sophisticated package for continual use.

The main reason we have included BT as an example of best practice is the imaginative array of transition support arrangements put in place to assist and guide those employees who had decided to take up the voluntary severance offer. Indeed, such was the success of the venture that the offer was oversubscribed initially, and a number of staff were told that, regrettably, it would not be possible for them to leave just yet! The various elements of the release programmes can be summarized under the following headings:

O   financial entitlements
O   employment initiatives
O   new lifestyle

O   training
O   self-employment
O   making a career change
O   self-help.

It is worth describing these elements of the programme in a little more detail.

FINANCIAL ENTITLEMENTS

Though a significant proportion of the leavers have been aged 50 and over (because of the immediate availability of a pension), the scheme has catered for employees of all ages and has been quite attractive to short-service personnel as well as long-serving staff. BT have introduced some very interesting options for people to choose from in this situation:

1   compensation lump sum payment based on length of service, with pension transferred to new employer's or personal pension plan, or deferred to age 60 (mainly for people aged under 50)
2   fixed lump sum payment, with enhanced pension benefits (for people aged 50 to 58)
3   as for 1, but with higher lump sum compensation payments based on length of service (for those aged under 50 with 10 to 14 years' service)
4   as for 1, but with fixed high lump sum compensation payment (for those aged under 45 with significant service)
5   lower fixed lump sum payment with enhanced pension benefits at 50, or higher lump sum payment with unenhanced pension at 50 (for those aged 45 to 49 with significant service)
6   as for 1, but with a higher lump sum payment (for those aged under 45 with substantial service)
7   special arrangements for those who joined before 1 December 1971.

It is clear that BT has taken great care to design a range of options to suit the differing circumstances of the employees deciding to go. These options are attractively presented in a booklet *Your guide to Release 93*, and are set out in a readily understandable form; this booklet is complemented by a companion volume *Release 93: Your questions answered*, which tackles aspects of financial entitlement under a whole range of circumstances.

EMPLOYMENT INITIATIVES

BT has adopted the Skillbase concept to provide certain employees with a bridge of temporary employment between leaving BT and starting a new career; it is one element in some of the packages described below. The basis of the scheme is that a resource company will offer employment of 60 days' work with BT. The company which deals with managers is the Skillbase company itself, and with nonmanagers the Manpower company is used. This arrangement has formed an important component of BT's overall strategy.

NEW LIFESTYLE

The new lifestyle package is open only to those aged 50 and over who are leaving and do not intend to continue in full-time work. It includes a new lifestyle workshop, in which the many activities that people can pursue, from voluntary work to leisure activities and education opportunities are discussed. The workshop also covers a number of practical issues including the importance of looking after one's health.

As part of this package staff are offered 10 per cent of pensionable pay to ease the transition into their new life. For certain individuals, they are also offered registration with a resource company (without guarantee of work, however) as part of BT's employment initiatives (described above).

TRAINING

Open to all employees, the training package is designed for people who are leaving BT and want to retrain in a different area of work. Advice and counselling is provided with regard to selecting the right course, and the cost of training fees for up to 12 months from the date of leaving, up to a given maximum, is met by the company. Again, registration with the resource company is also offered, without a work guarantee.

SELF-EMPLOYMENT

The self-employment package (also available) is designed for those intending to become self-employed and who feel that they need a high level of advice and guidance, which may represent the difference between success and failure in such a changed environment. Help is given in many areas, with answers to questions such as:

○   How marketable a product have I got?
○   How do I set up?
○   What about financing?
○   What about tax and VAT?
○   What are the legal requirements?
○   How do I prepare a business case?
○   Have I the ability to succeed?

As well as initial professional counselling and advice, continuing support is given in the first few months after setting up in business. A retraining grant is also available, up to a given maximum, payable on a 50/50 basis.

CAREER CHANGE

The career change package is for people who intend to find a new job with a different employer, again open to all employees. A retraining grant is available on a 50/50 basis, up to a given maximum. The main thrust, however, is through professional outplacement guidance and support in the following areas:

○ initial counselling
○ skill assessment
○ help preparing a c.v.
○ conducting a job search
○ how to tackle the interview.

In addition, selected individuals are offered a period of temporary employment with a resource company.

SELF-HELP

A cash payment of 10 per cent of pensionable pay is available to all employees who do not consider that any of the above options are tailored to their needs, and feel that they would like to pursue their own route when leaving BT.

The programme has undoubtedly been very successful, particularly regarding the voluntary nature of the releases. BT is pleased that the adoption of the Skillbase concept has been able to assist a considerable number of staff, which has given many the self-confidence to work on their own and to take advantage of the skills and experience acquired during their BT careers. To their surprise, there has been a significant demand for people with the training and specialist knowledge that they possess. In addition, BT has been able to bolster its work in the community by making use of selected people who applied for work through the resource company, which not only provided benefits for the projects involved but greatly assisted the employees in their transition from a main career.

There is now within BT a much better appreciation of the need for self-development, and a joint agreement between the manager and the individual to share responsibility for their personal development has become the norm; it is built into BT's annual performance and development review procedure. BT will provide financial support for training and education during an employee's career, given a work justification for the subject chosen. The release programmes have therefore stimulated a beneficial change in approach towards longer-term career orientation.

BT is noted for its commitment to working in the community, and it has been a prominent supporter of the Carnegie Inquiry into the Third Age (one of only a few employers who have demonstrated an active interest). It has sponsored a number of initiatives in connection with the employment part of the Inquiry, including a very productive seminar on the topic held at Wokeham Park in 1991 attended by one of the authors. BT's sponsorship in this direction has recently extended to the secondment of one of their senior executives, Richard Worsley (formerly Personnel Director, and latterly Director of Community Affairs), as Director of the Carnegie Inquiry. He has the task of causing the Inquiry's recommendations to be put into effect, which is likely to be achieved to a large degree through a carefully orchestrated communications campaign over a period of time. The authors hope that this book will make a contribution to this process by generating interest in Third Age issues among employing organizations.

BT has therefore not only contributed to this Third Age development by sponsoring events and research activities, but has seconded one of their executives to participate in the programme. This draws attention to the other side of BT's community work, in which a considerable number of their early retirers have become involved in working in the community in a wide variety of roles, such as assisting with local Enterprise Agencies, for example. This demonstrates the significant opportunity that a company like BT can offer to former employees, mainly as a facilitator through making advantageous use of the company and pensioner network.

13

IBM

❖

It is generally recognized that IBM has suffered worldwide as much as, if not more than, most corporations as a result of the recent recession. This, we believe, makes the story of how they tackled the situation particularly interesting. Though IBM's financial traumas in the US were widely reported, we understand that its UK subsidiary experienced a proportionately greater impact on its overall business. The main reasons were the dramatic changes taking place in the information technology industry which, exacerbated by the recession, created intense pressure on prices, costs and expense. The result was that changes that had previously spanned up to five or six years were happening in less than half that time and IBM's response had to match this acceleration. For a company which had a proud record of full employment, the idea of large reductions in staff was not a comfortable one but it was apparent that such reductions were an essential element in the range of restructuring measures required. The fact that they were achieved entirely on a voluntary basis and with minimal negative employee reaction is a tribute to the company's management.

In the UK, staffing was reduced from over 18 000 to less than 12 000 in around three and a half years; a reduction of over one third. This was achieved in several 'waves', each representing a specific campaign for stimulating voluntary separations. The associated financial and other arrangements were competitive by industry standards. However, it seems clear that less generous arrangements, although cheaper for the company, would not have achieved the desired results and would have been contrary to the ethos of IBM which has been such a major inspiration in its record of achievements. The corporation has been mindful of its image in the market-place as a leading employer and quality practitioner; one of the authors led a study tour of quality companies in Japan and the US, and IBM was automatically included as being one of the companies that *had* to be visited.

One of the main vehicles for achieving a significant volume of early retirements in the initial stages was the Skillbase arrangement in 1990. This has been described in some detail in Chapter 7 and will not, therefore, be repeated here. The way the company subsequently reduced its staffing was to start by determining, in each part of the business, the future resource levels required and, as a result, which areas of the company should participate in a given separation programme. Certain organizational groups of employees were excluded from the start by virtue of general skill needs and/or shortages. Once the potential release population was known, an appropriate programme was drawn up based on age, length of service and skill criteria.

The next stage was to send outline details of the offer to those employees in the eligible groups to elicit the level of interest. By definition, a proportion of those eligible would be allowed to leave if they so wished. In the most recent programme, the 'Skills Rebalancing Offer', employees who received details of the package were invited to complete a form indicating their level of interest as follows:

O   I would accept if offered
O   I am very interested
O   I am not interested.

Employees were given the opportunity to attend seminars in which the programme was explained in more detail and completing and returning the form did not represent a commitment by them to accept any offer which might eventually be made. Those expressing positive interest were interviewed to explore the opportunity in further detail.

Following reviews by management of those employees who continued to be interested, offers were made to individuals. Management reserved the right to make the final selection for offers based on an individual's specific skills and/or potential, so these offers represented a commitment by the company that those employees receiving them would be able to leave if they so wished. Having received offers, individual employees then decided whether or not to accept. It was only at this stage that the employee made a commitment to participate in the programme.

The Skills Rebalancing Offer document included the following information:

OFFER DESIGN

The offer incorporated two main aspects:

O   a lump sum payment
O   pension augmentation from age 44.

The money value of the offer shifted from lump sum to pension augmentation according to age. For employees near to or at pensionable age (50), the emphasis was on pension. Pension augmentation was achieved through a waiving of the actuarial reduction for specified ages and thus varied for each individual according to age and length of service. For younger employees a lump sum cash payment was the main ingredient but no one received a lump sum of less than one year's pay.

ELIGIBILITY

The offer was available to employees within specific organizational groups with a minimum of five years' service. As stated above, there is no guarantee that the offer will be confirmed for all employees in the eligible categories.

LUMP SUM PAYMENT

This was made up of three components:

O   past service element, generally based on one month's salary per year of service

O   future service element, related to a combination of years of service and age in order to compensate in some measure for future expectations that will not materialize

O   retraining element, consisting of a fixed lump sum to allow for a certain amount of retraining that might be necessary.

Reasonable limits for past and future service were built into the above arrangements.

PENSION DETAILS

The following categories were covered:

O   SRO pension window incorporating the facility to take early retirement or deferred pension from age 50.

O   pension augmentation for employees aged 44 and over via the use of an early retirement discount factor which reduced the number of years by which a pension is discounted (normally 3 per cent per year below age 60)

O   retiree benefits for those aged 50 and above who elected to take an immediate pension, including continuation in the IBM medical insurance plan, IBM club, retirement lunch/gift/seminar and accrued vacation entitlement.

OTHER BENEFITS

O   paid leave of absence

O   general information seminars covering offer design and content, financial and pensions advice

O   individual advice sessions providing one-to-one guidance on finance, investment and pensions

O   outplacement service on both a group and individual basis

O   opportunity to join the Skillbase freelance register

O   opportunity to purchase company car, where relevant.

Though the above is only an abbreviated summary of a thoroughly comprehensive document, it is possible to appreciate the scope of the benefits and the care taken to explain the offer in very great detail. Of particular interest, we believe, were the arrangements made for employees aged 44 and above. This must be one of the first schemes which has recognized that, even on a voluntary basis, not only the 50 year olds are within the target range at times of severe recession and radical restructuring. It is interesting to note that BT has followed IBM in this respect.

Those who left IBM's manufacturing operations were generally in the 50 plus age group reflecting the older nature of that population. In marketing and services, however, the average age of leavers was 46 indicating that a substantial number of younger people have been released from these areas. We understand that strenuous efforts were made to retain the critical skills needed both now and in the future by the final selection process for offers.

It is probably true to say that in the present environment, IBM, while attempting to take a longer-term, strategic look, has been distracted by the recent continuing need to reduce staff levels as quickly as possible. In fact, the company is a victim of its own success. A historical staff turnover rate of around 2 per cent provides little opportunity for 'natural' reductions. Consequently attention is being given to ways of minimizing the effects of this aspect by implementing such features as fixed term contracts for four or five years for new employees. It is also worth noting that IBM considers its links with its business partners e.g. customers, suppliers and agents to be a valuable potential outlet for certain employees who may wish to make a change. The company also uses secondments to support career transitions to mutual advantage.

The above offer illustrates, we believe, a pragmatic scheme of arrangements, applied in difficult circumstances, that demonstrate a very high level of professionalism in the face of the very difficult business situation in which the company found itself. It is clearly an example of best practice on which others are already building.

14

FORD

❖

Ten years ago Ford UK employed almost 80 000 people; this has since reduced to 30 000, yet the staggering fact remains that the number of cars produced each year has stayed much the same! Some large restructuring initiatives have been carried out in recent years, and progressive moves made to improve productivity, such as the well-known AJ (After Japan) campaign of a few years ago. Ford appear to be close to an optimum situation at the present time, given the level of technology that currently exists.

Ford has introduced some very interesting initiatives affecting mature employees during the past few years, some of them being unique to Ford and breaking new ground. These are in the fields of employee development, second careers, pre-retirement education and pensioner care, as described under each heading below.

EMPLOYEE DEVELOPMENT

Ford has an enviable reputation for training, which has always been an important feature in the company's background and history. It is hardly surprising, therefore, that the company should conceive one of the most imaginative forms of employee development that we have observed in our studies. It is called the Employee Development and Assistance Programme (EDAP) and is a joint initiative with the trade unions, established in 1987, with the first EDAP-funded course taking place in 1989. The basis of the programme is that every Ford employee is entitled to apply for one of the many training courses on offer, and the company will provide a grant of up to £200 towards the costs involved. The annual funding provided by the company was initially £1.8 million, and is now more than £2.2 million. The purpose is to enable Ford employees to develop themselves through learning new skills or enhancing their personal development.

The scheme would appear to have been a roaring success; literally thousands of employees have taken advantage of this positive opportunity, and the level of employee participation has been well in excess of 30 per cent, on a continuing basis. What is quite astonishing is that the training courses available cover a wide range of topics in the fields of education, business, the arts, health and leisure; the chosen courses and selected subjects are as varied as the individuals themselves. To illustrate this aspect, a breakdown of the 21,399 applications in 1991/92 by main subject is as follows:

Subject	% of applications
Education and academic	6.2
Languages	13.2
Business study and information technology	4.0
Music and performing arts	2.4
Arts and handicraft	3.5
Craft skills (construction)	11.0
Other skills (first aid)	11.4
Personal development	1.5
Health (aerobics)	18.0
Health (weight loss)	10.5
Leisure/sport	17.5
Other	0.8

As part of this programme some 240 employees are in the process of taking a degree, which is an impressive feature. In the context of Third Age transition the programme enables employees to extend their personal skills in a way that can match their needs and aspirations for the time when they will leave the company; there is a significant benefit in being able to do this earlier rather than later, as the programme is open to employees of all ages. The programme is administered through 22 local committees which cover all the Ford sites in the UK, and it can be regarded as a very significant national achievement in the field of employee development.

SECOND CAREERS – XR ASSOCIATES

When Ford were downsizing in the early 1990s, as part of their restructuring process, they wished to ease the transition of people aged 50 plus by using them on a part-time contract basis in appropriate roles. At the time two ex-directors of Ford decided to set up a company called XR Associates, which enabled this intention to be carried out in practice. Ford gave the company appropriate support by taking a minority shareholding in the company, as did IBM with Skillbase. The comments taken from their recent document express what we believe and endorse in a striking way:

> Patterns of work are changing rapidly as industry gets ready for the 21st century. Flexible working is set to increase as companies find that contracting out specialist work can improve efficiency and save costs. As companies shed employees in order to concentrate on their core business, so will they increasingly need to call on outside skills for specialist services, particularly for short-term assignments and peripheral activities, and to cope with temporary peaks in activity. Flexibility is the

key to future patterns of employment, and a growing proportion of companies expect to use more part-time workers and purchased services.

This statement emphasized one of the main themes in this book, which, as yet, appears to be recognized by few UK companies.

The founders of XR Associates, Don White and Eric Munday, have taken up the theme with enthusiasm, and have created a successful and developing business that has already achieved a turnover of some £10 million. It is a very specialized company, concentrating on specific product and service areas. The first batch of 200 managers (the grade applicable in this instance) joined the new company in January 1992; they were allowed to take a pension at age 50, and were normally offered 90 days' work for one year. Subsequently another batch of 25 managers joined in August 1992 (pension at age 55, 90 days' work), and another 150 managers in December 1992 (pension at 55, 45 days' work). In addition, some 150 engineers who had retired became available to Ford for part-time work through XR Associates. By these means, therefore, the new company had 545 professional staff on its books within a very short space of time.

During the past few years Ford has been reducing costs and improving effectiveness by introducing certain change programmes, frequently with the help of specialist consultants from the US. This process has been developed and extended by training associates in the relevant techniques, so that they are now able to lead and implement these important programmes themselves, not only in the UK but in Europe and the rest of the world. These projects are normally in one of three fields:

O   continuous process improvement (the Japanese 'Kaizen' approach)
O   value analysis of products, in conjunction with suppliers
O   value analysis and value engineering, for design.

Some 25 people are now employed by XR to carry out these programmes in Europe, currently working with Jaguar and other Ford divisions, and they are urgently looking for 25 additional specialists to join this venture. It is a measure of the success of this initiative that Ford are unable to meet XR's demands from internal sources, and they are having to advertise outside the company. XR also now manages the technical training services function on behalf of Ford, which is yet another string to their bow.

XR, in conjunction with Manchester Metropolitan University, are very interestingly looking into the motivations and personal responses regarding the flexible working arrangements experienced by the associates, and their future plans. The outcome from this research project should be quite revealing. It is XR's view that money is by no means the prime motivator; they feel that it is much more what the associates are doing that gives them satisfaction, and there seems to be little concern about taking on lower grade work. Being needed would appear to be the most significant motivator.

This highly successful activity has therefore been very beneficial not only to Ford but to the individuals participating in the project. The Director of Operations of XR told us: 'I've had only four days off this year, it's addictive you know', which just about summed up the accomplishment.

PRE-RETIREMENT EDUCATION

Ford has been active in the field of pre-retirement education for many years, and has participated in a number of corporate initiatives with other companies. There is currently both a general pre-retirement programme and a specific programme for managers, the average length of course being about three or four days. Taking advantage of the company's significant involvement in adult education through EDAP and other initiatives, Ford believes it now recognizes much more how people learn, and have concentrated on improving both the learning and the cost effectiveness of these programmes. Expensive hotels are 'out' and local pubs are 'in', with residential involvement kept to a minimum. Spouses are invited, and the aim is to cover potential retirers in their last year.

Ford has generally been somewhat dissatisfied with initiatives taken in collaboration with other organizations, so it has determined to 'do its own thing' and produce an interactive video on lifelong development. This is a highly significant development for Ford, since it addresses the issues involved in an entirely new way. The intention is to cover the following topics within this development:

O   financial planning
O   pensions and AVCs
O   education and leisure (linked to EDAP)
O   change, and adjusting to a new lifestyle
O   personal stocktaking
O   portfolio career opportunities, with relevant information.

The aim is to use this as a tool for open-learning centres, which are becoming a more prevalent feature within Ford. The advantage of this interactive video should be that the material could be taken up by an employee at any time. It should also be possible to use it in conjunction with a retirement planning course, so that the actual course could be shorter as well as being more productive. We await the outcome with interest.

PENSIONER CARE

Ford claims that it was the first company after Unilever to introduce post-retirement care many years ago. The Ford Pensioners' Association (FPA) was established in 1966 as a 'keep-in-touch' scheme. The FPA now has some 35 000 former employee members who are in receipt of a pension, and it operates a very active pensioner visiting programme. Pensioner visitors are volunteers selected from the ranks of retired staff, are paid expenses and aim to visit pensioners (and their widows or widowers) twice a year. There is a very comprehensive *Notes for Visitors* handbook, which outlines the main features involved in visiting and includes practical information for the visitor to use on such visits.

In addition there are Ford sports clubs in main locations in the UK, such as the Midlands, Southampton, South East, Halewood and Wales. These sports clubs provide opportunities for active pensioners to foregather and to initiate projects or outings as they see fit. The main benefit is that the pensioners are able to go somewhere where they feel they belong.

Ford appear to be innovative in a number of directions and give the impression of being more sympathetic to older people than many companies. For example, Ford is the first company we have met that refers to age in its Equal Opportunity statement. Under 'Commitment to Equal Opportunity' there is a paragraph as follows:

> The Company and the Trade Unions declare their opposition to any form of less favourable treatment accorded to Employees and Applicants for employment on the grounds of non-job related handicaps and unfair discrimination on grounds of age.

Though this is a statement that many firms would probably subscribe to, it is the first time we have found it in writing. In addition, employees are able to retire at age 55 with no actuarial reduction, and pension benefits are regarded as a priority feature by both the company and the trade unions. Consequently one gets the impression of a very business-like and practical approach to the issues of employment, career development and Third Age transition for mature people.

15

MARKS AND SPENCER

❖

Marks and Spencer has achieved an enviable reputation for quality throughout its operations, and particularly for the way in which it treats its staff.
This is especially the case when it comes to the development and career
transition of mature employees. Marks and Spencer currently employs some 52 000
people in the UK, and has 19 000 retired staff (likely to rise to 25 000 by the end of
the century). The company was one of the first to initiate pre-retirement education,
which it started 20 years ago for employees aged 55 plus. Three years ago it was
extended from only full-time staff (a two-day course with partner) to include part-
time staff (a one-day course). Though the normal retirement age is 60, the average
age of retirement for management is now around 55, similar to other organizations;
perhaps a more important objective for many, even today, is to reach 25 years'
service, as a symbol of achievement.

It is perhaps helpful to comment at this stage on the Marks and Spencer tradi-
tion of loyalty and long service, which makes it more difficult for staff to move away
from the company because of the strong emotional and psychological bonds
that exist. The company is now placing greater emphasis on self-awareness and
self-development to overcome this difficulty, so that people will become more
conscious of their personal make-up and aspirations in tandem with a traditional
allegiance to the organization.

Against this background, pre-retirement education was radically overhauled two
years ago to take account of changing circumstances, especially the increasingly
evident feature of early retirement. The company had found that the title of 'Pre-
retirement Course' was discouraging when it came to inviting people to participate,
so they changed the title to 'Planning for the Future', which seemed to be much
more appropriate. The programme consists of two distinct modules, for use at relevant ages, and covers both management and general staff (with minor modifica-
tions to the content in each instance). The main constituents of the modules are
given below.

PLANNING FOR THE FUTURE – PART ONE

Staff are invited to participate in this programme at age 40 to 45, and the object is to introduce people to the priorities of preparing for transition to the Third Age. This module mainly deals with financial aspects, covering the Marks and Spencer share scheme, pension scheme, advice on investments, but it also encourages participants to be more aware of the changing nature of employment. In the past people were told what to do; now the emphasis is on individuals' personal responsibility for their future lives and careers. This is a one-day module.

PLANNING FOR THE FUTURE – PART TWO

Part Two is for staff aged 50 plus, and consists of sessions which contribute to a genuine preparation for the Third Age. The topics covered include: coping with change, health awareness, DSS benefits, pension implications, a financial planning update, and a substantial session on 'new horizons'. The programme lasts for two days for managers and one day for other staff. An interesting feature is that former Marks and Spencer staff are invited to come and speak at appropriate sessions, which provides a reassuring link for the people concerned.

OPTIONAL MODULES

There are three optional, additional modules available to managers in their late 40s or early 50s which are currently being piloted within the organization. The main contents of each are as follows:

○   *Life planning*, which is a skills workshop lasting two days, covering identification of personal attributes and future needs, leading to the development of personal plans.

○   *Health awareness*, which deals with priority health issues, including stress management. It is a one day module; Marks and Spencer's in-house health services are highly developed, with a full team of medical staff employed by the company, and this is a follow-on from continuing awareness initiatives.

○   *New horizons*, which is a whole day devoted to consideration of the many opportunities that are available to people in their Third Age, and to exploration of personal inclinations and potential plans. It covers paid employment, starting up a business, operating as a consultant, working for a charity, or doing nothing!

There are a number of other initiatives Marks and Spencer has recently introduced, or are about to introduce:

○   *Telephone helpline* This special telephone helpline service was launched in 1991 for retired members of staff, and is available every weekday afternoon. This service has also been extended to employed staff who require information on 'Eldercare' issues. Fifty per cent of Marks and Spencer staff are over 40, so the mature population is considered to be a priority. The same concern applies to customers as well, and a project is currently under way to identify the shopping requirements of the older customer.

○ *Welfare fund for retired staff* There is a welfare fund provided by the company for use in circumstances of financial hardship to cover the costs of home repairs, heating bills, convalescent holidays, etc.

○ *Retiree volunteering* In this scheme volunteers will be released for one day a week in the lead up to retirement, as a preparation for a deeper involvement when eventually leaving the company.

Marks and Spencer can be identified with best practice because they have changed and adapted pre-retirement education to meet the very different circumstances caused by current economic and organizational developments; few companies have responded so quickly or imaginatively to the new situation. A feature that we liked particularly is that the company is aiming to 'break away from hidden agendas'. They want to reach the point at which staff will accept that Third Age transition can be talked about openly, and that going on a life planning or new horizons course doesn't imply that a career with Marks and Spencer is at an end. The company appears to be concerned to help people make the transition in the right way at the right time, which, in our view, is exactly how it should be.

16

PORTUGAL

❖

T here is a fascinating development that has taken place recently in Portugal. One of the authors has had a close association with Portuguese businesses since 1980, and he maintains a relationship with organizations in that country. These Portuguese associates expressed a great interest in the activities of Future Perfect, and asked for a study to be carried out to examine how the situation of mature employees in Portugal might best be addressed. Seven companies contributed to the initial review in 1991, and it soon became apparent why the companies were so interested in the potential difficulties with mature employees. An analysis of the data provided showed that 42 per cent of their workforce were aged over 45 (compared with 25 per cent in the UK) and 4 per cent were aged over 55.

These figures therefore demonstrated that, though the proportion of employees over 55 were perhaps not causing immediate concern, there was a time-bomb ticking away which needed defusing. The organizations concerned became particularly aware of the opportunities that would become available if something similar to the Skillbase operation in the UK could be introduced in Portugal. They were very interested both in the savings that could be achieved through releasing people from the payroll on an attractive voluntary basis, and in the imaginative ways in which former employees might be used in their former place of work and as consultants in the open market. Consequently further exploration was carried out to determine what practical steps could be taken, and to assess the measure of support that might be available for any appropriate action put forward.

Thus began a series of discussions between the interested parties involved, which resulted in a draft business plan being developed during the course of these consultations, to interpret the ideas generated by this process. It was an exciting time, because the Portuguese are quite different to the British, and wanted to create something unique to Portugal that would go beyond anything that had been developed elsewhere. They wanted to initiate a commercial company with the following characteristics:

O   Each company would contribute to the equity of the company, and would thus become an active stakeholder in the venture.

O   Provision would be made for the Chief Executive and other leading executives also to take an equity stake to enhance their commitment.

O   Each contributing company would provide appropriate mature managers who would be taking early retirement to become core members of Talent Pool (an English name chosen by them!). They would be entitled to a given amount of work on a part-time basis with their former company.

O   The company would set out to offer consultancy services both within the shareholder companies and on the open market.

O   Talent Pool would also aim to attract professional men and women with relevant skills and experience from other sources to join as members, in order to build up the scope of its consulting capability.

The business plan produced to embrace all these ideas was greeted with acclaim, and the enthusiasm was such that ten companies ultimately sponsored the venture as shareholders. They are:

O   Solisnor, a company involved in the construction and management of ships and shipyards

O   CTT, the Portuguese telecommunications authority

O   TAP, more commonly known as Air Portugal, the Portuguese airline company

O   Imperio, one of Portugal's largest insurance companies

O   IPE, the State holding company for a large number of Portuguese medium-size businesses

O   Soresfame, a mechanical engineering company

O   Lisnave, the well-known ship-repair firm based in Lisbon

O   Mague, a company manufacturing cranes and lifting gear of all kinds

O   IBM, the Portuguese branch of the multinational corporation

O   TLP, the Portuguese telephone company.

There were thus ten companies that were prepared to back this imaginative venture. They were very fortunate that a prominent and well-respected business figure, Ricardo Cabrita, was enthusiastic to lead the new company as President and Chief Executive. He was formerly President of Quimigal, the country's leading chemicals company, and a Director of Lisnave, the ship-repair company that is one of Talent Pool's principal sponsors.

Talent Pool was launched internally among the sponsors on 20 May 1992, and to businesses at large on 13 October 1992. The October launch was promoted by, amongst others, a government minister, Dr Isabel Maria Corte Real, who gave a stimulating and supportive address. The event was attended by a significant proportion of Portugal's senior executives from a wide range of companies. The company now operates on a commercial basis from a suite of offices in central Lisbon, with a small staff, and is carrying out some very interesting projects for Portuguese clients. The membership in the initial stage stands at around 150 professional business people, who have a high degree of enthusiasm, and it is growing steadily as the concept becomes more widely known and appreciated.

We believe that the Talent Pool arrangement has a number of very positive features to it, and is quite unlike any other organization that we have met. Its principal advantage would appear to be that it has the solid support and commitment of a chosen number of sponsors. These companies can thus communicate between themselves and, in collaboration with Talent Pool, can make optimum use of Third Agers in Portugal with relevant qualifications for specific projects. By these means the companies have a wonderful opportunity for releasing their managerial and professional staff into an organization which will continue to service them, thereby yielding considerable savings, whilst stimulating and assisting the individuals to realize their aspirations for the Third Age.

APPENDICES

❖

APPENDICES

APPENDIX I
THE STORY OF FUTURE PERFECT

❖

A small working group of people with notable business, personnel or academic backgrounds started to meet in 1987. The group had been brought together by John Ottensooser, a senior financial adviser with Allied Dunbar, who had a vision about the potential of the Third Age for each one of us, in contrast to the negative connotations of retirement. He wanted to explore how this vision could be translated into providing practical support for individuals approaching their Third Age, to stimulate and encourage the positive aspects of transition. The group included Professor Charles Handy of the London Business School, Parry Rogers, Chairman of BTEC and formerly Personnel Director of IBM and Plessey, Dennis Stevenson, Chairman of SRU, Director of Pearson and Chairman of the Trustees of the Tate Gallery, and Barry Curnow, then Chairman and Chief Executive of MSL International.

The group soon came to appreciate the powerful implications of the issues they were considering; the social and economic trends involved pointed to the emergence of a potentially critical situation for the UK in the future, affecting both companies and individuals in significant ways. These perceptions were well in advance of public awareness or recognition by corporations of the changes that would materialize progressively over the next decade.

The group believed that provision of relevant Third Age transition support could form the basis of a new business. Such a business would not only be able to make a valuable contribution to the UK managerial and professional population (the initial target), but should also be able to provide a financial return on the funds required to mount the activities involved. Consequently a suitable business plan was drawn up with the help of Arthur Anderson and Co., funds pledged by group members as share capital, and a potential chief executive sought to launch the new company. It was decided to call the company 'Future Perfect', following an inspiration by John's wife, Sheila.

Various preparatory moves to create the new business were made during 1988, and John McLean Fox, a Director of the PA Consulting Group, was appointed Chief Executive, to commence on 1 April 1989. The new company came into operation at that time, with a staff of two, John Lumbard and Jean Marzetti. The official launch of the company came a little while later, on 24 May 1989, and took the form of a reception at the City of London Club with some 100 guests. The gathering was addressed by Parry Rogers, Future Perfect's first Chairman, by John McLean Fox, its Chief Executive, followed by a launch endorsement from the Right Honourable Michael Heseltine, MP, who felt that an appropriate message to Third Agers was 'Past tense, Future Perfect'. The company thus started off with widespread support for the underlying concept and the objectives outlined.

The Board, which consisted mainly of the original working group, decided that the company's target market should consist initially of managerial and professional staff in large corporations, and that the service offerings of Future Perfect should address this specific population. The company therefore started to carry out appropriate research and develop suitable products for this market, the content of which forms much of the material to be found in this book. The first Future Perfect workshop for individuals and couples was held in September 1989, based on development work carried out by John McLean Fox with the help of Jinny Ditzler and Gary Davies, specialist coaches in the personal development field, and Derek Hill, now Head of Counselling at Relate. The methodology launched and developed through these initial workshops provided the foundation for Future Perfect's subsequent workshop and counselling activities, carried out principally with the help of associates Greta Colman, John Downs, Maggie Hammond, and Brian Morton. Barry Curnow, a founder director, became Chairman in 1991, and Future Perfect continues to make progress in assisting both companies and individuals to deal with significant career transition issues. The company is about to enter a new phase of development on this front in order to capitalize on the substantial experience already gained in this specialist field.

APPENDIX II
AGE AND EMPLOYMENT: AN IPM STATEMENT

AGE DISCRIMINATION

Age discrimination in employment occurs as a result of prejudice, misconception and stereotyping which hinders the proper consideration of an individual's talents, skills, abilities, potential and experience.

Arbitrary age discrimination in employment can affect everyone. It consistently disadvantages older workers, young people and women returners. It consistently favours individuals in the age group twenty-five to thirty-five. Decisions based on age are rarely justifiable, are frequently of poor quality and lead to the ineffective use of human resources.

OBJECTIVES OF THE STATEMENT

The purpose of this statement is to encourage personnel policies and practices which lead to the productive employment of people, irrespective of their age.

It sets out a number of recommendations to prevent the misuse of age and age bands in employment.

It amplifies the reference to arbitrary age discrimination in the IPM's Equal Opportunities Code.

LEGISLATIVE BACKGROUND

With the exception of the protection afforded under the Sex Discrimination Act 1986, Chapter 59, Section 3, there is no legislative protection against age discrimination in the United Kingdom.

Initiatives to make it illegal to use age in job advertisements and to adopt legislation similar to that which exists in the United States, have been unsuccessful.

The IPM recognizes the enforcement value of legislation as a possible way forward, but currently favours self-regulation.

THE IPM VIEW

Irrespective of the issue of legislation, the IPM holds the view that a national campaign and training are essential to increase the awareness of employers, employees and their representatives about the implications of age discrimination.

The prevention of age discrimination requires raised awareness of the issues through information and education, behavioural change based on the adoption of best employment practice and attitudinal change through better understanding and training.

The development and promotion of a positive approach to best employment practice is the key to changing behaviour and attitudes about age and age related criteria in employment. A set of recommendations for personnel policy makers and practitioners follows.

THE BUSINESS IMPLICATIONS OF AGE DISCRIMINATION

The IPM believes that the effect of unfair age discrimination in employment is a bottom line business issue and undermines effective human resourcing. Better decisions about people and work can be made by removing the use of age and age related criteria and adopting the use of objective criteria related to satisfactory job performance.

Against the background of the changing mix of the labour market, which includes an increasing number of people aged forty plus (by the year 2000 it is estimated that one person in three in the labour force will be aged over forty) and a proportionately smaller number of young people, the IPM believes that it is a business imperative for employers to review their personnel policies, practices and procedures to prevent the inappropriate use of age and age related criteria in all employment decision making.

Organizations which fail to do so will be considerably disadvantaged in their quest to develop a competitive edge in the market place.

Some of the implications which affect employers, individuals and society include

O   Inefficient and ineffective human resourcing.
O   Under-utilization of key sectors of the labour market, particularly young people, older workers, women returners and mature graduates.
O   Distorted collective bargaining power for 'privileged' labour in the favoured age groups.

KEY FACTS ABOUT AGE AND AGE DISCRIMINATION

O   Age is a poor predictor of job performance
O   It is misleading to equate physical and mental ability with age.
O   A greater number of the population are living active, healthy lives as they get older.
O   There is an increasing number of older workers in the labour market.
O   Age is rarely a genuine employment requirement.
O   Society's attitudes may encourage compliance with outmoded personnel practices regarding recruitment, promotion, training, redundancy and retirement.
O   Reduced self-confidence, self-esteem and motivation, together with loss or reduction of financial independence for individuals and their dependants are some of the harmful effects of age discrimination.

AGE DISCRIMINATION AND THE EMPLOYMENT CYCLE

Arbitrary age discrimination can be both overt and covert and occur directly and indirectly at all stages of the employment cycle, including:

O   Job definition
O   Job/person specifications
O   Recruitment procedures, including advertising, sorting and sifting application forms, curriculum vitae, shortlisting, selection interviewing and selection decisions.
O   Training, including induction, career development, skills training and counselling
O   Appraisal
O   Promotion
O   Pay and remuneration packages
O   Retention, redundancy, termination and retirement.

RECOMMENDATIONS FOR REDUCING AGE DISCRIMINATION IN EMPLOYMENT

KEY SUGGESTIONS

O   The use of age and age related criteria should be challenged in every aspect of employment decision making, for example, in recruitment, selection for training, counselling, development, promotion; as a determinant of pay and as a criterion for redundancy.
O   Equal opportunities policies and practices should include a commitment to remove arbitrary age discrimination and promote the adoption of job related criteria for all employment decisions.

○   All staff, particularly those making employment decisions, should be educated and trained about the business and human resource implications of age discrimination.

○   Dates of birth should be used only for monitoring purposes. Written statements to this effect should be made to gain the confidence of individuals and the commitment of staff making employment decisions on behalf of the organization.

○   Monitoring should be carried out at regular intervals to find out whether or not there is any indication of unfair discrimination against particular age groups.

○   Positive action policies should be considered to encourage individuals in age groups subject to disadvantage, particularly in relation to recruitment, training and career development.

○   Age, age guidelines and age related criteria should not be used to exclude particular age groups.

Bearing these key suggestions in mind, each stage of the employment cycle should be examined as follows.

Recruitment and selection

○   *Advertising*. The use of age, age related criteria or age ranges in job advertisements is not recommended unless clearly identified as positive action to attract more individuals from an under-represented age group. It is important not to use age in job advertisements to exclude particular age groups. The purpose of job advertisements is to attract the best qualified candidates for satisfactory job performance. It does not make good business sense to deliberately exclude suitably qualified candidates on the basis of age.

○   *Application forms*. It is desirable to state that age criteria will not be taken into account in employment decisions (except where, in very exceptional circumstances, age can be shown to be a genuine occupation requirement).

○   *The selection interview*. Interviewers and those concerned with selection decisions must be aware that subjective, stereotypical views about age are dangerous, as is judging an individual's age on the basis of physical characteristics or appearance.

Medical advice

An individual's age should not be used in order to make judgements about their physical abilities or medical fitness. Where such a judgement is required, an occupational health or medical practitioner should be consulted.

Remuneration

Pay and terms and conditions of employment should generally not be based on age or age related criteria but should reflect the degree to which an individual meets the required standards of satisfactory job performance and the value of their contribution to the overall objectives of the organization.

Training and development

It is inefficient to automatically exclude particular age groups from training and development programmes. Training programmes which are geared to the needs of older workers help them to successfully acquire new skills.

Reorganization, retention and redundancy

The future needs of an organization regarding particular knowledge, skills and competencies should be taken into account when decisions about the retention and redundancy of individual employees are made. Both long and short term implications should be considered.

It is important to remember that older workers tend not to change jobs as frequently as young employees and correspondingly offer good potential return on employment and training investment.

Using age criteria for redundancy selection can lead to unnecessary and undesirable loss of the talents and skills which are essential to the organization.

Retirement

With the greying of the workforce and changing demographics, the issue of flexible retirement will come to the forefront. New ways will need to be established to harness the talents and skills of older workers, who may or may not wish to cease employment at the normal or statutory age. Flexible decades of retirement have already been mooted and new taxation laws facilitate the continued employment of older workers beyond the age of normal retirement. Greater use of flexible working and reduced hours will need to be considered for employees who have a preference to alter the balance of their working and personal lives. This will be an important business issue for employers seeking cost-effective and efficient ways of using people's skills as the labour market mix continues to change.

The efficient and effective use of people's skills requires that employment decisions should be based on competencies, qualifications, skills potential and objective job related criteria obtained through the careful analysis of job requirements and satisfactory job performance.

The use of age, age bands, age guides and age related criteria reduces objectivity in employment decision making. It increases the likelihood of poor quality and inappropriate decisions which are harmful to individuals and wasteful of people's skills.

The foregoing statement on
Age and Employment is
reproduced by kind permission
of the Institute of Personnel Management.

REFERENCES

McLean Fox, J. (1990), *'Attracting and motivating the financially secure employee'* presented at IPM National Conference, Harrogate.

Haworth, Dr. J. (1993), 'Working to live: Having a Job Seems to be Necessary for Self-esteem', *The Times*, 24 September.

Carnegie Inquiry Reports (1993), 'Life, Work and Livelihood in the Third Age', London: The Carnegie United Kingdom Trust.

Handy, C. (1989), *The Age of Unreason*, London: Arrow Books.

Harrison, M. (1577), *Description of Britain*.

Institute of Personnel Management [IPM], (1993), 'Policies, Attitudes and Practice towards Age and Employment', an IPM report.

Kantor, Rosabeth Moss (1989), When Giants Learn to Dance.

Kinsman, F. (1990), *Millennium 2000*, London: W.H. Allen.

Sheehy, G. (1976), *Passages*, New York: Bantam Books.

Sheehy, G. (1982), *Pathfinders*, New York: Bantam Books.

Towers Perrin, (1990), 'Priorities for Competitive Advantage', London a study for IBM.

RECOMMENDED READING

Open University, The (1982), *Planning Retirement*, London: Choice Publications Ltd.

Allen, J. and Pifer, A. (1993), *Women on the Front Lines*, Washington DC: Urban Institute Press.

Bolles, R. N. (Annually), *What Color is Your Parachute?*, Berkeley, CA: Ten Speed Press.

Brown, R. (Annually), *Good Retirement Guide*, London: Kogan Page.

Directorate-General for Employment, Industrial Relations and Social Affairs. (1993), *Social Europe 1993: European Year of Older People and Solidarity between Generations*, Brussels: Commission of the European Communities.

European Community Observatory (1991), *Social and Economic Policies and Older People*, Brussels: Commission of the European Communities.

Erikson, E. H. (1977), *Childhood and Society*, London: Paladin.

Golzen, G. (1989), *Going Freelance*, London: Kogan Page.

Green, C (1992), 'Making the Most of Older People at Work', an MA dissertation.

Hopson, B. and Scally, M. (1991), *Build Your Own Rainbow: a Workbook for Career and Life Management*, London: Mercury Business Books.

ICAS, (1993), *EAPs and Counselling Provision in UK Organisations 1993: an ICAS Report and Policy Guide*.

Laslett, P. (1989), *A Fresh Map of Life: the Emergence of the Third Age*, London: Weidenfeld.

Levinson, D.J. (1978), *The Seasons of a Man's Life*, New York: Ballantine Books.

Maloney, T. W. and Paul, B. (1989), 'Enabling Older Americans to Work' in *1989 Annual Report of the Commonwealth Fund*, New York: The Commonwealth Fund.

OECD (1992), *Employment Outlook: July 1992*, Paris: Organisation for Economic Co-operation and Development.

OECD (1988), *Ageing Populations: the Social Policy Implications*, Paris: OECD.

Schuller, T. and Walker, A. (1990), *The Time of Our Life: Education, Employment and Retirement in the Third Age*, London: Institute for Public Policy Research.

Smith, M. (1992), *Changing Course*, London: Mercury Business Books.
Coulson-Thomas, C. (1989), *Too Old at 40?*, London: Institute of Management.
Young, M. and Schuller, T. (1991), *Life After Work: the Arrival of the Ageless Society*,
    London: HarperCollins.

INDEX

Essential Health and Safety for Managers
A Guide to Good Practice in the European Union

Ron Akass

Managers are employed for their professional expertise, which may not include familiarity with workplace health and safety. Nevertheless, the avalanche of health and safety regulations introduced as a consequence of the Single Market is exposing managers to a real risk of contravening them, which can have serious personal consequences.

This book, written for all managers of people, shows how health and safety can become intuitive, an everyday part of the workplace routine that is an integral part of the job, and not an appendage to it.

- Part One covers the fundamentals of health and safety, including the Health and Safety at Work Act 1974 (HASAWA) which remains the UK's primary health and safety legislation, notwithstanding the EC-driven regulations.
- Part Two describes legislation made under HASAWA before 1993 which is applicable to most businesses. In this part there are chapters dealing with key health and safety matters – fire, accident reporting and COSHH – as well as a composite chapter covering a number of regulations, which are simply explained.
- Part Three deals with the six sets of regulations enacted under the aegis of HASAWA to give effect to EC Directives. These regulations already apply although there are transition periods in which to achieve full compliance for three of the six. Each regulation is covered in detail in a separate chapter.

At the end of each chapter, 'Management action checklists' contain questions which enable the reader to review the principal requirements of the regulations or subject covered.

1994   288 pages   0 566 07332 3

Gower

Making the Most of Action Learning

Scott Inglis

Here at last is a book on action learning designed to be read by non-specialists. Drawing extensively on case histories and "real life" examples, the author:

- describes what action learning is and how it works
- shows how to bring action learning into an organization
- discusses the benefits to be expected and the costs involved
- explains how to avoid common pitfalls.

Unlike much of the existing material on action learning, the emphasis here is on the needs of the organization, whether in the private or the public sector. The main model used is that of an in-house action learning programme designed to tackle issues of critical importance to the organization.

For any manager wanting to know what action learning can do for his or her organization, Scott Inglis's new book is the ideal guide.

Contents

1994   246 pages   0 566 07452 4

Gower

The
Motivation Manual

Gisela Hagemann

Improved productivity, flexible work practices, low rates of absenteeism, commitment to quality, ever-higher standards of customer service -these are the benefits of a well-motivated workforce. In this prize-winning book the author takes modern motivational theory and shows how any manager can apply it to create shared vision, develop mutual trust and involve employees in the decision-making process.

The text is enlivened throughout by examples with which managers will identify and there is a unique final section containing twenty seven exercises designed to strengthen interpersonal skills and improve creativity.

Contents

1992   210 pages   0 566 07295 5

Gower

Professional Report Writing

Simon Mort

Professional Report Writing is probably the most thorough treatment of this subject available, covering every aspect of an area often taken for granted. The author provides not just helpful analysis but also practical guidance on such topics as:

- deciding the format
- structuring a report
- stylistic pitfalls and how to avoid them
- making the most of illustrations
- ensuring a consistent layout

The theme throughout is fitness for purpose, and the text is enriched by a wide variety of examples drawn from the worlds of business, industry and government. The annotated bibliography includes a review of the leading dictionaries and reference books. Simon Mort's new book is destined to become an indispensable reference work for managers, civil servants, local government officers, consultants and professsionals of every kind.

Contents

Types and purposes of reports • Structure: introduction and body • Structure: conclusions and recommendations • Appendices and other attachments • Choosing words • Writing for non-technical readers • Style • Reviewing and editing • Summaries and concise writing • Visual illustrations • Preparing a report • Physical presentation • Appendix I Numbering systems • Appendix II Suggestions for further reading • Appendix III References • Index.

1992   232 pages   0 566 02712 7

Gower

The Prosperity Handbook
Winning the Money Game

Paul de Haas and Surya Lovejoy

In this book, the authors propose a deal with the reader. They promise that:

- You will experience a dramatically increased level of prosperity;
- You will discover the source of all financial problems, including your own;
- You will develop new, empowering and effective ways of relating to the four facets of money: earning, spending, saving and investing

In exchange, the reader is asked to complete fully all 42 steps in order to maximise their gain from the book.

The Prosperity Handbook is for anyone who wants more money than they have now – but it's not about making money. It is for anyone who wants a powerful new way to plan and manage their finances – but it's not about financial planning. It is for anyone who wants to learn about successful approaches to handling money – but it's not a money advice book.

The Prosperity Handbook is about relating to money as a game in which aiming to win is essential for success and satisfaction. The step-by-step programme includes tools designed to provide new and effective approaches to earning, saving, spending and investing. The object of the programme is to develop in the reader a new relationship to money in which they have power, control and freedom, together with a real sense of prosperity.

1994   160 pages   0 566 07447 8

Gower

35 Checklists for Human Resource Management

Ian MacKay

*In association with the Institute of
Training and Development*

The late Ian MacKay started producing his checklists in the early years of his work as a lecturer in human resource management. They reflected his view that the role of the lecturer is not so much to teach as to help others to learn and, above all, to think for themselves.

From 1985 onwards, Ian MacKay's checklists were a regular - and outstandingly popular - feature of the Institute of Training and Development's journal. A collection in book form, *35 Checklists for Human Resource Development*, was published in 1989 and has found an appreciative, and steadily growing, readership. This companion volume covers a wide variety of human resource issues, from apparently mundane tasks like designing application forms to issues of the utmost sensitivity like appraisal, grievance-handling and redundancy policy.

As in the previous volume, the checklists are not designed to provide easy answers. What they will do is help you to think in a structured way about your attitudes and behaviour. Your responses can then become a basis for increasing your effectiveness.

Personnel specialists, and others involved in human resource management, will find working through the checklists a challenging and rewarding exercise.

1993   184 pages   0 566 07433 8

Gower

Training Needs Analysis
A Resource for Identifying Training Needs, Selecting Training Strategies, and Developing Training Plans

Sharon Bartram and Brenda Gibson

This unique manual is designed as a practical tool for trainers. It contains 22 instruments and documents for gathering and processing information about training and development issues within your organization. This frees you from the time-consuming business of formulating methods for generating information and allows you to concentrate instead on the all-important task of making contacts and building relationships.

Part I of the manual examines the process of identifying and analysing training needs. It reviews the different types of information the instruments will generate and provides guidance on deciding how training needs can best be met. This part concludes with ideas for presenting training plans and making your findings and proposals acceptable to others.

Part II contains the instruments themselves. They cover organizational development, organizational climate, managing resources and job skills. Each section begins with an introduction which defines the area covered, describes the instruments, and identifies the target groups. It also provides a checklist of the preparations you will need to make. The instruments themselves represent a wide range of methods, including card sorts, questionnaires, profiles and grids.

Effective training requires a serious investment in time and finance. This manual will help you to ensure that the investment your organization makes will achieve the desired results.

1994   200 pages   0 566 07561 X Hardback   0 566 07437 0 Looseleaf

Gower

The Zen of Groups
A Handbook for People Meeting with a Purpose

Dale Hunter, Anne Bailey and Bill Taylor

- Understanding groups is an essential skill for anyone who's part of one: this book explains how to get the most from any group.
- 'Thinking Points' and 'Toolkit' exercises challenge assumptions and involve the reader.

Increasingly the work of organizations is being carried out by groups rather than individuals. Moreover, all of us belong to groups throughout our lives – families, school, community, education and recreation groups. This book is designed to help you become a more effective member of the group and to show how the effectiveness of the group itself can be greatly increased. It offers insight into what makes groups work powerfully, and teaches through practical advice and numerous exercises.

The Zen of Groups is in two sections. The first nine chapters explain how groups function and put forward a number of ways for improving their performance. Throughout the text, 'Thinking Points' ask a series of questions designed to challenge the reader's assumptions.

The second section consists of a 'toolkit' containing 95 techniques and exercises for developing group effectiveness. The exercises are indexed under eighteen headings, ranging from *Tools for generating ideas* to *Tools for ending and evaluation* to enable the reader to select the most appropriate.

The Zen of Groups is written in an informal style, and based on the authors' experience of working with a wide range of groups over many years. It will be of immense value to facilitators and group members alike.

1994   200 pages   0 566 07486 9

Gower